ANGELS
Heaven Helping Us

Unless otherwise indicated, all scriptures are quoted from The King James Bible.

Scripture quotations marked (NKJV) are taken from the New King James Version. Copyright © 1982 by Thomas Nelson, Inc. Used by permission. All rights reserved.

Scripture quotations marked (The Message) are taken from *The Message*. Copyright © 1993, 1994, 1995, 1996, 2000, 2001, 2002. Used by permission of NavPress Publishing Group. www.navpress.com

Scripture quotations marked (NLT) are taken from the Holy Bible, *New Living Translation*, copyright © 1996, 2004, 2007 by Tyndale House Foundation. Used by permission of Tyndale House Publishers, Inc., Carol Stream, Illinois 60188. All rights reserved.

*Kenneth E. Hagin, *I Believe in Visions*, 2nd ed. (Tulsa, OK: Faith Library Publications, 1984), pp. 119–123. Used with permission. www.rhema.org.

Scripture quotations marked (AMP) are taken from the *Amplified® Bible*, Copyright © 1954, 1958, 1962, 1964, 1965, 1987 by The Lockman Foundation. Used by permission. www.Lockman.org.

ANGELS
Heaven Helping Us

978-1-6803-1474-8

Published by Harrison House Publishers
www.harrisonhouse.com

Copyright © 2012 by Mark Brazee. Printed in the United States of America. All rights reserved under International Copyright Law. Contents and/or cover may not be reproduced in whole or in part in any form without the express written consent of the author and publisher.

CONTENTS

Introduction 5

Chapter 1 – Modern-Day Angel Testimonies. 9

Chapter 2 – What Angels Are All About. 27

Chapter 3 – Angels Through the Bible 41

Chapter 4 – God's Enforcers of Protection 55

Chapter 5 – Angels Deliver Healings and Miracles . . 67

Chapter 6 – Divine Connections, Guidance 79
        Encouragement and More

Chapter 7 – Angels Bring in the Money 103

Chapter 8 – Don't Be Fooled by False Angels 117

Chapter 9 – Angelic Reapers of Harvest 123

Chapter 10 – Activating Angels in Your Life. 135

INTRODUCTION

God has made a lot of promises to mankind. He's made a lot of promises to you and me, and one of the primary ways God keeps His promises and delivers the help mankind needs is through the avenue of angelic activity.

Angels are here to help heaven help us.

It's been true all through the Old Testament, it's been true all through the New Testament, and it's true even now as we bump up against everything God is beginning to do in this hour.

God worked through angels in the Old Testament delivering protection and victory on the battlefield, showing up with hosts of angelic armies and chariots of fire. Angels brought supernatural provision and food as three million children of Israel traveled to the Promised Land. An angel closed the mouths of lions ready to attack Daniel in the lions' den and rescued Shadrach, Meshach and Abednego from the fire.

In the New Testament, angels announced the birth of Jesus, His ministry and His resurrection from the dead. Angels broke Peter out of jail and stood by Paul during a violent storm and ship wreck. And when the trumpet sounds, angels will announce the return of Jesus in great glory.

Yet, what angels have done for mankind from Genesis to Revelation is only the beginning. Angels are all around us today continuing to work in our lives. The Bible tells us in Matthew 18:10 that God assigns a guardian angel to each human being, so whether you have seen an angel or whether you ever do see an angel makes no difference. Either way, I guarantee you that angels are working in your life.

In fact, even now God's Word gives us every reason to believe we're about to see a flurry of angelic activity on the earth. I believe this increase of angelic assistance is about to unfold before us and surpass every Bible account we've read and every testimony we've heard. Why? We're entering an era when the Church is preparing to do its greatest work, experience its greatest miracles and need its greatest assistance.

Let's purpose to know more about God's angels so we can expect their help and not be afraid when God has them manifest in unusual ways. Let's partner with angels assigned by God to work hand in hand with us bringing about God's will in the earth and in our lives. How? We need to develop an accurate picture of angels and what they're all about. We need to recognize who they are, what they are, and when and how they function. We need to understand how we can cooperate with them and activate them in our lives.

In the chapters that follow, we'll share scriptural foundations and eye-witness testimonies of how angels are assigned to guard and protect us, deliver healing and miracles to us, bring in money to meet our needs, arrange divine connections and appointments for us, provide us directions and guidance and much more.

Keep in mind that these mighty supernatural angelic creatures are not the chubby little babies wearing diapers and shooting bows and arrows we see on Valentine's Day cards. They're also not the females in long white flowing gowns we see in museum paintings around the world. The angels I'm talking about are the same big, powerful beings the Bible talks about.

It's important that we don't get excessive or extreme on the topic of angels and worship them or elevate them ahead of the Lord Jesus Christ Himself. In more than 30 years of ministry, I've seen so many times when angels would begin to manifest, but before long they became all people could think about and talk about. Angels don't take the place of Jesus or the Holy Spirit. They don't take the place of God's Word or faith or prayer. But they are one facet of how God ministers and a facet the Church needs to know more about and understand.

If the Church will allow angels to manifest and work in our behalf without worshipping them, then we will experience their help like never before. That's why we need these truths planted in our hearts and stirred up in our lives. At times we'll know when angels are working with us; most of the time we won't. But mark my words, we will see results, and we'll thank God for it. Angels will be actively involved in harvest and in so many different areas of our lives.

Let's expect their help.

Let's expect them to be involved in our lives and in our churches.

Let's expect *angels to help heaven help us.*

—Mark Brazee

Chapter One

Modern-Day Angel Testimonies

It's so important in this day and age for us to talk about angel activity and share personal testimonies and eye-witness accounts from others about the working of angels. It stirs up a great expectation and opens the door for angels to work more and more in our lives.

My wife, Janet, and I can testify to angels at work in our lives and ministry many times over the years. Since 1979 Janet and I have traveled to at least 50 nations of the world, making more than 150 trips. We've been places we probably shouldn't have been, but we've always had a bold and supernatural confidence that God was taking care of us.

We've gotten off trains in the middle of the night in major European cities long before suitcases had wheels. We hooked up our luggage carts, piled on the suitcases and headed down streets looking for hotels no matter the time of night. At times we didn't have money for taxis, and even when we did, we didn't speak the language and didn't have a way to tell the driver where to take us.

If our parents had known some places we traveled, they probably would still be cringing to this day. Yet, we always believed without a doubt that God had given His angels charge over us, keeping us in all our ways. We didn't intentionally make unsafe choices; we just did not always have other options. We were scheduled to be certain places to teach the gospel, and we were doing what it took to obey God and go where He sent us. The one thing we knew for sure was that angels were traveling with us—and they weren't chubby little cherubs either. We had big, powerful angels watching over us then, and we have big, powerful angels watching over us now.

Asleep at the Wheel

From the time I got saved in November 1972, I've always been conscious of angelic help. I knew angels were taking care of me even before I got saved because I had folks who prayed for me and prayers avail much. But one particular occasion in college was the first time I knew for a fact that God assigned an angel to save my life.

I was attending college in East Lansing, Michigan, when I got saved and not too long afterward came spring break. My roommate and I jumped in the car and said to each other, "Where are we going?" We didn't really care where we went as long as we found warm weather, so we decided to drive south. We got on I-75 and away we went. A few states later, we hit sunny weather and hung out for as long as we could.

Eventually we had to hurry back for college classes the next morning, so we jumped in the car with only a nap and planned to drive all night. My roommate drove for awhile and then said, "I'm climbing in the back seat to sleep. You drive for awhile."

"Not a problem," I said. At some point, however, I started getting drowsy after staring out the dark windshield for hours. Still, I had my hands on the steering wheel the proper way as usual. But the next thing I knew, I felt my elbow jerk sharply; the entire car jerked sharply! I was horrified when I realized that I had fallen asleep while driving the car.

When the car jerked so forcefully, I woke up startled. The thought, *We're in trouble!* flashed through my mind. Worse yet, when I realized we were driving down the middle of the lane *after the jerk*, I realized just how bad things really had been. It dawned on me that if the car jerked and moved, and yet at that point we were headed correctly down the road, then apparently we had been headed wrong and dangerously out of the lane before I woke up startled.

Seconds later I glanced up ahead and saw a big overpass. We must have been headed right straight for the concrete overpass when *something* grabbed my elbow, jerked the car and got us back in the lane. What do you suppose that was? I suppose it was an angel assigned by God to keep us alive and get us back to school safely.

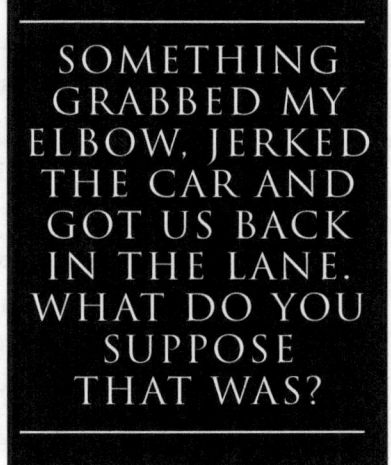

SOMETHING GRABBED MY ELBOW, JERKED THE CAR AND GOT US BACK IN THE LANE. WHAT DO YOU SUPPOSE THAT WAS?

Back Seat Driver

A number of years later, driving across country from Florida to Kentucky, I did the same thing again. I was driving along by myself, and before long I started getting sleepy, but figured I could push myself to drive another couple of hours. All of the sudden I felt my arm jerk, and then the whole van jerked. I realized I was on a hilly road and must have been headed in a bad direction. When I jerked I ended up right back in the lane where I should have been.

This time I heard the words, "Don't make me do that again!" Thank God for the angel who straightened out the car and woke me up. I appreciate my angel and all the work he's done in my life, but I don't want to push it. That was 1978, and I have not fallen asleep on the road since then. Right then I remembered the scripture, "Thou shall not tempt the Lord thy God" (Deuteronomy 6:16). Since then Janet and I have logged lots and lots of miles driving on the road, but when I get drowsy, I stop.

Angels Directing Traffic

In the early 1980s, an angel helped us on the highway once again. Traveling as itinerant ministers, we were on our way to the Wisconsin area where someone had offered to book the month of December for us. That was great news since December isn't typically a good month for traveling ministers because most church calendars are busy with Christmas activities. So back then if we were offered a December meeting, it didn't matter where it was, we quickly accepted the invitation.

A person had contacted us and said, "If you'll come to Wisconsin, we'll set up two solid weeks of meetings for you all in one location." Unfortunately, they had to call back and explain they ran into some problems. Long story short, the whole schedule fell apart. "But I've rebooked you," the person said. "You still have a full schedule."

The interesting part was that when we got to Wisconsin, we realized the meetings had been scheduled back and forth across the state. A meeting was on one side of the state one night and clear across the state the next night. Then the next night we were back to the other side and then back again. In other words, we were routed all over the state of Wisconsin crisscrossing back and forth.

Let's just say we did not have an ideal itinerary, and we did not have ideal driving conditions either. There's a lot of desolate territory up there once you get out of the cities. It was also *really, really* cold—record cold. With the wind chill factored in, it was something like 60 degrees below zero.

This was a big surprise to my lovely wife from Louisiana. When she said her wedding vows she repeated, "Withersoever thou goest, I'll go. Thy God shall be my God." But back then, she had no idea what she was getting herself into when she married me. When we walked outside that December, she said, "Oh! My nose hairs have frozen!" I had a mustache at the time that seemed to turn into a big icicle in under 10 minutes flat. No joke. It was cold. We would drive our car an hour or two, but still not have any heat. I mean it was **cold**.

We prayed for divine protection as we drove across the state night after night in the dark. You could drive for miles and not see a light, not see a house, not see anything. I believe sometimes God covers for us when we don't use a lot of smarts ourselves or when there are no options. Still, we didn't worry about how dangerous it would be if our car broke down; we just thanked God for divine protection.

I still remember the night we were on a two-lane back road hurrying to the other side of the state, and God mightily protected us. Out of the corner of my eye, I saw a deer running out of the woods headed straight for us. It would have meant a major crash. Then amazingly, the deer ran to the side of the road and began spinning in circles. We drove right by the deer going round and round and round in circles.

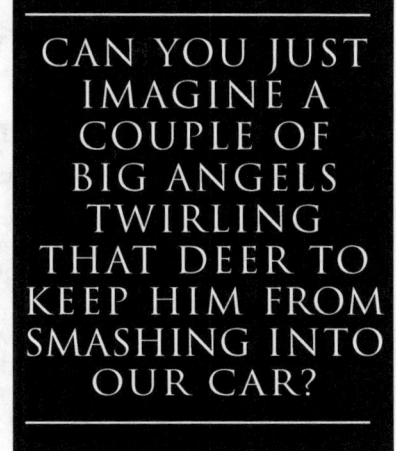

> CAN YOU JUST IMAGINE A COUPLE OF BIG ANGELS TWIRLING THAT DEER TO KEEP HIM FROM SMASHING INTO OUR CAR?

Can you just imagine a couple of big angels twirling that deer to keep him from smashing into our car? That poor deer probably wondered what in the world he just ran into when he met up with our angels. God's angels were on the scene working to keep us safe.

Angels on the Mission Field

On my first overseas missions trip in 1978, I traveled with another minister to Kenya, South Africa. We were covering two countries in just a few weeks, so we had flown from Tulsa to New York, caught another flight in New York to London and arrived in the morning with a seven-hour time difference. We spent the first day in London sightseeing and then returned to the airport to catch a night flight to Nairobi. By the time we got into Nairobi, we hadn't slept in about two days.

We were in for a surprise because for some reason we had thought we were traveling to a major city. But we got off the plane and were greeted by two Kenyan ministers carrying a sign with our name on it. After fellowshipping with the ministers for a few minutes we asked, "Are we going to our hotel now?"

"No," the Kenyan ministers said, "Now we take you over to the taxi stand. We put you in a taxi (more of a van), and you go six hours on a trip through the Rift Valley to a place called Kisumu."

"Really?" we asked. "We've got six or seven more hours through the Rift Valley?"

It was a gorgeous place with giraffes running across the terrain. But after two days without sleep, we were almost too tired to see anything, so we asked, "Is there any other way to get there?"

"There's another small airport here, and they have small planes. We could probably get somebody to fly you over there," they said.

"Let's go find out," we said.

So they put us in a car, took us to this other private airport and found an Australian bush pilot with a single-engine four-seat plane.

"Can you fly us to Kisumu?" we asked him.

"Sure," he said.

We figured out the price, paid him, and filled the plane with luggage so there was barely enough room for the two of us to sit with the pilot. Even then, the Kenyan ministers took about half the luggage down to the taxi stand and strapped it to the top of a vehicle. We were novices at traveling at that point, and clearly we had way too much luggage.

Sitting in the back seat of the plane with suitcases piled next to me, I was reminded of the "Gilligan's Island" S.S. Minnow with its three-hour tour. But at least we were airborne and on our way, so I lay back and slept soundly. All of a sudden, I felt the plane bank sharply to the right, and I woke right up.

"What's going on?" I asked.

"There's a storm over at the Kisumu airport," the pilot said. "I can't land there."

He didn't say anything else so I fell back to sleep. We flew a little while longer when suddenly we were descending in the middle of a field surrounded by trees and woods. There was no airport, no tarmac, no luggage carousels. Still, right in the middle of these desolate surroundings, the plane landed, and the pilot turned off the engine.

Before we knew it, the pilot hauled the suitcases out of the plane to the side of the road, which really was more of a path with a couple of ruts. He lined up the suitcases saying, "It's getting dark, and that storm is coming this direction. I've got to get out of here!"

"I'll tell you what," he added. "You guys hitchhike on that road into Kericho. Have the guy take you to the Tea Hotel. When you get there, you can get a taxi to take you to Kisumu. Gotta go. See ya. Bye."

Minutes later he had fired up the plane and headed off into the sunset. The other minister and I had no idea where we were; we didn't even know for sure we were still in Africa. The pilot got his money, and he was off. We didn't have a clue where we were, and he didn't tell us.

We decided to walk toward the road, which was great except there were no cars. Finally we saw a mini pick up truck coming with a shell on the back of it, but the guy drove way around us and kept driving. Dark clouds were forming, and the storm was coming closer. It wasn't a pretty picture.

Finally another little vehicle came by, and we held up our thumbs, but that driver only sped up and raced around us. By then the sky was really dark, and things were looking even worse. We looked at each other and said, "We probably ought to get in faith over this." So we said, "Lord, we really need a ride to Kericho, wherever Kericho is. Thank You, Lord, for a ride." Still we could see no more vehicles on the road.

All of a sudden a man came walking out of the woods who appeared to be a Kenyan. He walked directly up to us and said in perfect English, "May I help you?" Yeah, I think so.

"We need to get to Kericho. Do you know where that is?" we asked.

"Yes," he said.

"We need a ride."

"OK," he said.

About that time another vehicle comes down the road. The Kenyan from the woods didn't give the thumb sign like we had. He just stepped out into the middle of the road, and sure enough, the driver pulled over and talked to our friend from the woods.

He came back and said, "He will take you to the Tea Hotel in Kericho for such and such amount of money." It wasn't much at all.

"Great!" we said as we counted out the money and climbed into the back of a truck with four or five Kenyan guys. The guy from the woods took our suitcases and tied them on top of the truck, and we were ready to roll. As we sat down, he just waved and walked back into the woods.

"Thank you!" I hollered.

> "OH, MY BROTHERS WE HAVE A MIRACLE!" HE SAID. "OH, WE HAVE A MIRACLE!"

About an hour later, we ended up at the Tea Hotel in Kericho and began the last leg of our journey by taxi to Kisumu. Eventually, we arrived at our hotel in Kisumu and met our contact, Brother Silas Owete. He was a wonderful man who warmly greeted us in the hotel foyer, asking, "My brothers, my brothers, where have you been?"

We told him what happened, and the more we talked the bigger his eyes got.

"Oh, my brothers we have a miracle!" he said. "Oh, we have a miracle!"

"We have?" we asked.

"Oh, yes," he said. "You must understand the place where you were dropped off is filled with people who normally would kill you and take your luggage. It's not a good place to be, my brothers. There are visitors who go there every now and then, but they are never seen again. Normally, we would have found your goods all over the countryside. It's a miracle, my brothers, a miracle!"

Right then I was saying, "Dear Jesus, thank You for divine protection." We were in a potentially very dangerous place, and we didn't even know it. And yet, I believe the Kenyan man who came out of the woods was an angel of God. I'm convinced that he was sent to deliver us, and he probably saved our lives. I'm sure I've met that guy in different forms all over the world because we've had God help us in so many places.

Angels Put the Brakes On

Angels have traveled with us for years, and we've never had to buy them a single ticket. They've flown with us on airplanes, driven with us in cars and ridden with us on buses. In fact, I remember riding a bus down steep hills in the middle of the Philippine Islands on one missionary trip when I realized the brakes had gone out on the bus. The driver hit the brake pedal all right, but I watched it slap against the floor and lay there *flat*.

Meanwhile, we were racing down the hill at full speed. Get the picture in your mind for just a minute: big hill, bus full of people, no brakes. But, praise God, all of a sudden the brakes started working because God's angels were on the scene taking care of us. Angels were unseen forces protecting us and saving our lives.

Angel Saves Pastor's Life

I remember another story of angels at work in the Philippines. A friend of ours was ministering in a large church in Manila, Philippines, and saw an angel sitting in the balcony. The angel told the minister, "Tell the pastor that I saved his life at such and such a place."

The minister turned to the pastor and said, "There's an angel up in the balcony right now. He just told me to tell you that he saved your life." The minister quoted the time and the place that the angel had given.

"Well, the angel is exactly right. I remember the time and the place," the pastor said. "I didn't know it was an angel who saved my life, but I knew something supernatural had happened to help me."

Angel on Guard in the Train Tunnel

I'm so glad that angels are not limited by passports or airfares or countries or locations. Two young women from our church traveled to Mongolia on a missionary journey a few years back and were grateful for an angel who protected them in a train tunnel.

One of the young women shared her testimony with our church. She prefaced her testimony by explaining that she had learned first-hand that when two young women travel to a foreign country and don't know anyone or the language, the stage is set for adventure.

She said they witnessed for themselves that the environment in Mongolia seemed "raw" by some standards and that in many instances visitors to the country were often robbed. "There were stories that natives would put their hands in purses or try to grab visitors," she said. "We heard reports of taxis taking people places they didn't want to go and reports of people wandering the streets in violence and desperation."

The young woman explained that on this particular trip the two of them were taking a train to another city near the Russian border, but couldn't figure out how to make their connections. "We showed our ticket to people and did lots of pointing; missions work can be a lot like charades sometimes," she said. "We finally realized we were totally in the wrong area on the wrong side of the tracks. To get to the other side, we had to take a tunnel underneath the train tracks."

The young woman continued her story: "Loaded up with our heavy backpacks on our backs, we headed down the stairs. It was really dark and dreary down there and pretty desolate. The only person we saw was a big man in the shadows leaning against a back wall.

"The minute he saw us, he began walking toward us. Immediately, we knew his intentions weren't good, so we locked arms and braced ourselves. We were carrying 50-pound backpacks, and we couldn't have run even if we had wanted to run."

"'*What do we do? What do we do?*' we began whispering to one another.

"The really troubling part was that if we moved to one side, he also moved to one side. If we shifted the other way, he did too. He was heading straight for us without stopping. Finally, he got to within about six inches of our faces and stopped like he hit a brick wall. The man got a really strange look on his face and began looking two or three feet above our heads.

"His eyes still focused way above our heads like he was looking up at somebody, he said in perfect English, 'Oh, excuse me. I am sorry.' Then he simply walked away.

> ANGELS ARE ON ASSIGNMENT BY GOD TO PROTECT US WHATEVER WE'RE CALLED TO DO AND WHEREVER WE'RE DOING IT.

"Shocked, we immediately turned around to see what tall person behind us could possibly have frightened the guy off. We saw no one. Then it dawned on us, 'Angels!'

"We realized an angel had come to our rescue and was more than enough to send the guy with bad intentions packing. God was protecting us even when we didn't know what was going on!"

Angel in Uniform

Angels don't just show up to protect missionaries on the field or ministers traveling to preach the gospel. Angels are on assignment by God to protect us whatever we're called to do and wherever we're doing it.

In fact, this is a female police officer's testimony of how an angel in uniform protected her from danger one night while on duty:

"While on routine patrol one night on the midnight shift, I pulled up to a traffic light on a busy street with a drinking establishment on one corner. At the unction of the Holy Spirit, because God is a God who loves justice, I saw a car light come on in the parking lot. As soon as I saw those headlights come on, the Holy Spirit said, 'Stop that car.'

"Of course, in law enforcement you have to have probable cause to stop a car, so I was sort of watching the car and following it a ways. I took a right to get in behind this fellow driving a big, old Buick LeSabre. It was almost two decades ago now, but I remember it like it was yesterday.

"After his car weaved left of center, I thought, *Ah-ha, a drunk.* He saw me in his rear view mirror and made a sharp left, but he didn't use his turn signal. *Ah-ha, failure to signal,* I thought, *There's my probable cause.*

"Long story short, I pulled the car over and told communications over the radio that I was out on a vehicle stop. All of a sudden a big foot—and I mean enormous foot so much bigger than almost anyone's—kicked open his car door and out came a massively huge guy. I'm only a little over five feet tall and almost everybody seems tall to me anyway.

"I thought, *Dear God in heaven, I've just stopped the Brawny man with a twist of Grizzly Adams.* He must have been 6'4" and had a lot of meat on him. The guy was massive.

"So as he's climbing out of his car, I got on the radio and told communications, 'Start me a backer.' But eventually I had to get out of my car because I didn't want Brawny-man coming back to me. I screamed at him to stick his hands out and turn around. When he did I saw a pistol in his waistband.

"*Yikes!* I thought.

"'Lord,' I said out loud, 'What have You gotten me into?' I was serious because it was the Holy Spirit that told me to pull the guy over in the first place.

"So I tell Brawny-man, 'OK, now you've really got to keep your hands out to the side.'

"As I walked up to him again, I said, 'Headquarters, you've got to get me a backer started.' But all I heard from the dispatcher was, 'I'm trying.'

"Suffice it to say, I got the gun away from Brawny-man and put it in the back of my waistband, but I still had to manage to handcuff him and search him again. So I got him down on his knees and even on his knees he was almost my height.

"I stood there thinking, *Holy cow, I've got to search this guy. Lord, how do I do this?* So I got on the radio one more time and in my frustration said, 'Headquarters, *please*, send me a backer!'

"To that Bozo the clown Brawny-man said, 'What's wrong with the one you've got?' As he said this to me, his eyes were huge like 50-cent pieces.

"I don't know where the words came from that fell out of my mouth next except that they came from my spirit. I didn't plan them. I wasn't thinking them because when I looked behind me, I was aware of nothing. But I heard myself say, 'He's a rookie, and he likes to fight.'

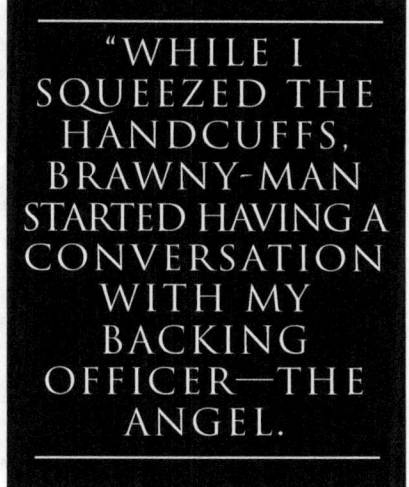

"WHILE I SQUEEZED THE HANDCUFFS, BRAWNY-MAN STARTED HAVING A CONVERSATION WITH MY BACKING OFFICER—THE ANGEL.

"Just hearing myself say that made me think, *What?!*

"Brawny-man said, 'Well, I wouldn't mess with him.'

"About this time, I realized Brawny-man had to be seeing an angel that God sent to help me. It's probably a good idea that I didn't see him because I really believe it would have distracted me, and I did have Brawny-guy there to deal with. I had to search him, and I pulled two more guns off this guy while I was trying to fit handcuffs on him. His wrists were like as big as my calves, and I had to squeeze and *squeeze;* finally they locked.

"While I squeezed the handcuffs, Brawny-man started having a conversation with my backing officer—the angel. This is how the conversation went. Keep in mind that Brawny-man was in trouble, but he was not drunk. He did not get arrested for DUI. He got arrested for a felon in possession of firearms. As I ran his record, I found out the guy had a rap sheet as long as I was tall with arrests for firearms, homicides, sexual assaults, assaulting police officers and on and on and on.

"As I finished patting the guy down, he looked over my shoulder and said to the angel that I could not see, 'Boy, I know you didn't walk into the uniform shop and pick that uniform off the shelf. You're way too big. I know they don't make them that big. Where did you get that uniform? Is that special made?'

"Then Brawny-man looked at me and said, 'He doesn't say much, does he?'

"To which I replied, 'He doesn't need to.'

"Needless to say, I got him cuffed and up, and the guy was completely compliant. I walked him over to his car and leaned him over it because I had to search his vehicle all by myself—but not. I pulled three more guns out of his car, and then I got a sawed-off shotgun out of his trunk with about 220 rounds of ammunition. This guy was trouble.

"But I'll tell you this right now, as surely as the Lord lives, the uniform on the angel wasn't for the benefit of Brawny-man; it was for me because I had been so frustrated at not getting a backer. I mean, Brawny-man was like 6'4," and yet he looked up at my angel. The man's eyes were huge as he looked at the angel, and whatever I wanted him to do, he did it. He did it because the presence of God was with me in the form of that angel, and I realized that I have the only backer I will ever need."

Angel Offers Roadside Assistance

I heard another testimony recently about a young woman who drove through a city and got lost. She ended up in an area where she really shouldn't have been, a really rough part of town known for crime and violence. Worse yet, her car broke down and just stopped. She was really afraid because she recognized it was no place for a young woman to be alone.

But seemingly out of the blue, a very nice car pulled up behind her and a well-dressed man in a business suit got out and said, "You're in the wrong place!"

"That's for sure!" she said.

He gave her directions. Then he raised the hood of the car, did a little something, and the car instantly started. Before she knew it, he closed the hood of her car and got back in his car. She looked back to say thank you and wave at him, but both the man and his car had totally disappeared. How's that for supernatural, angelic road-side service?

> EVERY ONE OF US SHOULD BE AWARE OF DIVINE SERVICE ROADSIDE AND EVERY OTHER SIDE. OUR ANGELS ARE ALL AROUND US ON ASSIGNMENT.

Angels can and will do all kinds of amazing things to take care of us. Every one of us should be aware of divine service roadside and every other side. Our angels are all around us on assignment. Your angel is no scrawny little guy; he's big and strong. Your angel has been around forever, he's well seasoned, well trained and ready to show up whenever needed.

Angels Directing Traffic

I remember a number of years ago, Janet was scheduled to speak at a women's meeting in the Florida panhandle. The women on our ministry staff were excited about the meeting, so we rented a van to allow them to attend the conference.

Janet was scheduled to fly down later, but the women left about 5:30 a.m. one morning facing a 14-hour drive. All of a sudden that morning I woke up very early thinking, *I really don't have any reason to get up at this time.* I'm not what you call a morning person, but I lay there for a second realizing I had an unction to pray. Something just didn't seem right.

I lay there quietly praying in other tongues for about an hour. The urgency didn't seem to be extremely strong, but yet there was a burden to pray. After awhile I hit a place in prayer where the burden lifted, and

I felt peaceful and happy inside. I began to laugh, and I got a release. As quick as it came, the burden lifted.

I didn't think a lot of it, but I asked, "Lord, what was that about?"

Sometimes He'll tell you; sometimes He doesn't. This time He answered me. As clear as could be, I heard the Spirit of God say, "The devil is going to try to take your staff out today, but he won't be able to now." I thought, *Thank God for the Holy Spirit.*

Before Janet left for the meeting, I told her what had happened and I said, "Just keep your ears open. See if you hear anything in particular. Maybe the staff will never even know."

Janet arrived in Florida and was checking into the hotel about the time the staff ladies arrived. She asked the women about their trip.

"It was really good," one of the gals said.

"Anything unusual happen?" Janet asked.

"Well, yeah," one of the women answered. "We were driving down the highway behind a vehicle in the passing lane on a two-lane interstate, but suddenly the vehicle slammed on its brakes for what appeared to be no reason at all."

"Problem was," she continued, "there was no way for us to stop. We were too close to be able to put on the brakes. The vehicle in front of us was passing another vehicle, so we had two cars in front of us with nowhere to go. But somehow—amazingly enough—we fit three vehicles in two lanes."

"I have no idea how," our staff member said, "We went between those two vehicles with our full-sized van. We got through the middle and didn't touch either one of them. We were so overwhelmed that we made it to the other side that we pulled off the road and cried."

What happened? I've always been well persuaded that some big, strong angel somehow got between those two vehicles and pushed them aside just enough to get that van through the middle and safely to the other side. I believe the women on staff are alive and well today because the Holy Spirit alerted us to pray. Perhaps He alerted many people to pray, and as a result of prayer, God assigned angels to direct highway traffic and protect our staff.

Chapter Two

What Angels Are All About

The Church world as a whole has been fad-oriented and sidetracked by many things that have come along through the years. In fact, the Church has been famous for jumping into ditches on various topics throughout history, and we've had a difficult time staying in the middle of the road on just about everything. Some folks tend to grab hold of certain half truths, and before you know it, they're off in never-never land. That's definitely been the case on the topic of angels.

There have been times when a report about an angel has come to the forefront, and then all the sudden people begin talking about angels, angels, angels—everything angels. They lose sight of the fact that our Christian walk isn't all about angels—it's all about Jesus Christ.

Yet, I believe God wants us to find the middle of the road and stay in the middle of the road on the topic of angels because we're about to experience a great increase in angelic activity. Angels may not appear to all of us, but they will help us and cooperate with us whether we see them or not. We can lay important ground work for angels to manifest more often by understanding who and what they are and who and what they are not.

The Rank of Angels

Look with me at Hebrews 1 to examine basic, foundational truths from God's Word that will help us better understand how to cooperate with angels.

Hebrews 1:1-4

1 God, who at sundry times and in divers manners spake in time past unto the fathers by the prophets,

2 Hath in these last days spoken unto us by his Son, whom he hath appointed heir of all things, by whom also he made the worlds;

3 Who being the brightness of his glory, and the express image of his person, and upholding all things by the word of his power, when he had by himself purged our sins, sat down on the right hand of the Majesty on high;

4 Being made so much better than the angels, as he hath by inheritance obtained a more excellent name than they.

> WE CAN LAY IMPORTANT GROUND WORK FOR ANGELS TO MANIFEST MORE OFTEN BY UNDERSTANDING WHO AND WHAT THEY ARE AND WHO AND WHAT THEY ARE NOT.

In these scriptures the writer of Hebrews, most likely Paul according to most Bible scholars, is teaching early Christians who had recently become saved and come out of Judaism. They had come out of their particular religious background and culture, switching from the old covenant to the new covenant and learning more about Jesus, the way, the truth and the life. But obviously God knew these believers needed a few things prioritized for them. The new Christians knew God from the old covenant. They knew angels from the old covenant, but they needed to understand where Jesus stood in light of it all.

God moved on the writer of Hebrews to instruct these early Christians by explaining, "Don't get confused about the rank of angels. Jesus is far above angels." Most Christians today hear this and think, *Well, yeah.* But these newly saved Hebrew Christians didn't have the New Testament to read like we do.

Skipping down a few verses in the chapter, the Bible begins to offer proofs that Jesus ranks higher than angels.

> **Hebrews 1:5-8**
>
> 5 For unto which of the angels said he at any time, Thou art my son, this day have I begotten thee? And again, I will be to him a Father, and he shall be to me a Son?
>
> 6 And again, when he bringeth in the firstbegotten into the world ... he saith, And let all the angels of God worship him.
>
> 7 And of the angels he saith, Who maketh his angels spirits, and his ministers a flame of fire.
>
> 8 But unto the Son he saith, Thy throne, O God, is for ever and ever: a sceptre of righteousness is the sceptre of thy kingdom.

Now notice verses 13-14 of the same chapter.

> **Hebrews 1:13-14**
>
> 13 But to which of the angels said he at any time, Sit on my right hand, until I make thine enemies thy footstool?
>
> 14 Are they not all ministering spirits, sent forth to minister for them who shall be heirs of salvation?

Verse 13 continues making the point that Jesus is elevated above angels by asking the question, "Which angel did God invite to sit at God's right hand?" The answer is not one.

Then verse 14 drives home the point that Jesus is not only above some angels, but also He's far above "*all* ministering spirits." The Bible is clarifying that Jesus is above every classification of angel such as—seraphim, cherubim and archangel. That means Jesus is also far above archangels Michael and Gabriel, and definitely above Lucifer. Jesus is far above every name that is named. He's above angels.

He's above principalities and powers. He's above you and me. He's far above. Period.

Another important point comes to light about angels in verse 14. Notice the latter half of the verse says, "Are they not all ministering spirits, sent forth to minister for them who shall be *heirs of salvation?*" Who are the *heirs of salvation?* That's us—the Church or the body of Christ. It refers to the born again, the blood-bought, the redeemed.

There's not a certain category of angel that is above us and a certain category that is below us. No. Here's how God prioritizes things. Jesus comes first. Then comes the Church. Then come the angels. The Church is below Jesus because He's the head of the Church, but as the Church, we are a step above the angels.

A Little Lower Than God

In Hebrews 2 we learn even more about God's ranking of angels. Verses 6-7 say, "…What is man, that thou art mindful of him? or the son of man, that thou visitest him? *Thou madest him a little lower than the angels…."*

These New Testament verses actually quote Psalm 8, which says:

> **Psalm 8:4-5**
> 4 What is man, that thou art mindful of him? and the son of man, that thou visitest him?
> 5 For thou hast made him a little lower than the angels, [elohim] and hast crowned him with glory and honour.

The margin of most Bibles references the word *elohim* for the word *angels,* which is how it reads in the original Hebrew language of Psalm 8. But translated literally the scripture reads, "God, you made him a little lower than Yourself" or a little lower than God.

Notice the difference again. The King James translation of Hebrews 2:6-7 says, "You made him a little lower than angels." But the original language of Psalm 8 literally says, "God, you made him a little lower than Yourself." The point is that the Bible never said that Christians were a little lower than the angels; it said we were made just a little lower than God Himself.

We're made from the very substance that God Himself is made, and He breathed His life—*Himself*—into us. God's own Spirit—eternal life—resides inside every born again Christian. We are a spirit; we have a soul; we live in a body. God is also a spirit, so when God created man, He made him in His own image and in His own likeness. That's not how God created angels.

> HERE'S HOW GOD PRIORITIZES THINGS. JESUS COMES FIRST. THEN COMES THE CHURCH. THEN COME THE ANGELS.

When you get a hold of the prioritization that God Himself set up, then it's easy to understand why angels should not be worshipped or highly magnified. Are angels assigned by God with power to help us? Yes! Do we welcome their help? Yes! And we're in a prime position to receive their help if we'll just remember that angels must remain in the background while Jesus Christ must remain in the foreground.

The Purpose of Angels

Now that we're clear on the rank of angels in God's system of priorities, let's focus more on the purpose of angels. I believe God wants us to know enough about angels—who they are, what they do and why they are—so when they manifest more and more in our lives in the days to come, we won't get confused about them.

"What is it that God created them to do? What is their job?" somebody asks. Actually, we just saw their purpose in Hebrews 1:14. "Are they not all ministering spirits, *sent forth* **to minister for** *them who shall be* **heirs of salvation**." Angels are ministering spirits created by God;

they are not born like men and women. They are created beings whose purpose is to serve God and help believers.

Too often our mentality is, *Wow—angels showed up, and they're of greater value, greater power, greater dominion, greater authority, greater everything than we are as human beings.* But that's not true; that's not Bible. God said Jesus is far above angels and so is the Church, and the primary job of angels is to minister **to** and **for** us. So angels are not here on earth for us to minister to them and to worship them. They're assigned by heaven to work hand in hand with us.

Stir yourself up right now and begin to expect angels to work in your life. After all, you just read that angels were created to minister to you and for you. God's Word confirms beyond a shadow of a doubt that there are unseen angels around you all the time assigned to help you at every given moment.

> GOD'S WORD CONFIRMS BEYOND A SHADOW OF A DOUBT THAT THERE ARE UNSEEN ANGELS AROUND YOU ALL THE TIME ASSIGNED TO HELP YOU AT EVERY GIVEN MOMENT.

Somebody might ask, "How come some people see angels and know they're helping, but other times people don't seem to benefit from angels at all?" Scriptures tell us that the level of assistance we receive from angels depends directly on our learning to cooperate with them and learning to activate them in our lives.

I think a lot of us have had someone else's prayers activate angels in our lives in times past, so we're not as familiar with how to obtain their help. Yet overall, whether or not we know angels are present and helping us, has nothing to do with whether or not they *are* helping us. Then again, many times I believe angels sit around with nothing to do because nobody gives them a job to do, which we'll talk more about in Chapter 10.

Assigned to All

For certain, each of us is the responsibility of at least one angel. The Bible tells us that God assigns a guardian angel to each human being. Angels live down here on earth with us all the time. In fact, notice what it says in Matthew 18:10, "Take heed that ye despise not one of these little ones; for I say unto you, That in heaven *their angels do always behold the face of my Father which is in heaven.*" Angels are assigned to us at the beginning, and they remain with us until the end.

I remember that angels were at work in the life of my niece Rachel's little daughter, Ava, when she was only a few hours old. Ava was born premature and experienced some pretty serious challenges in the beginning of her life. Doctors didn't give her much chance of surviving, but a lot of people were praying, believing God and speaking the Word over her. That's why she's alive and well today.

But family members had said as tiny as she was that she would lie in the hospital crib with her little eyes open looking around the top of the room. I believe she might have been seeing angels because plenty of people were assigning angels in her behalf by praying and speaking God's Word over her.

Even now that she's a little older, Ava ran to get her mom one day and said, "Mom, I want you to see the guy in my room."

"Well, who is it?" her mother asked almost jokingly.

"He's a big man dressed in white," Ava answered. "He was right there!" she said pointing to a chair.

Maybe Ava is still seeing angels.

The Bible tells us that angels are not only at the beginning of life, but they're also at the end of life. Psalm 73:24 says, "Thou shalt guide me with thy counsel, and afterward receive me to glory." We understand from this scripture that angels are involved in receiving or escorting believers to heaven when it's time to step over to the other side.

Don't ever feel sorry for a believer who dies. I don't believe any born-again Christian experiences death because we've already passed from death to life (John 5:24). A person's heart may stop, but I don't believe he or she experiences the pains of death. When a Christian dies, he or she simply sheds the body and changes locations to a new home in heaven.

I remember when my grandmother was in her 90s she was getting to where she couldn't get around. She had begun to get a little confused now and then, and ultimately, she went into a nursing home for a few weeks.

At one point she told my aunts about an important visitor who came to see her. "There's been a nice young man standing in that corner right over there for about three days. He keeps waving at me," she said. "I think I'm going to go with him." Within a couple of hours, she just smiled and went over to heaven.

"That's a nice story," somebody says. "But have you got scripture to back it up?" What about Luke 16 where Lazarus was carried into Abraham's bosom.

> **Luke 16:19-22**
>
> 19 There was a certain rich man, which was clothed in purple and fine linen, and fared sumptuously every day:
>
> 20 And there was a certain beggar named Lazarus, which was laid at his gate, full of sores,
>
> 21 And desiring to be fed with the crumbs which fell from the rich man's table: moreover the dogs came and licked his sores.
>
> 22 And it came to pass, that the beggar died, and was carried by the angels into Abraham's bosom: the rich man also died, and was buried.

We just read that when Lazarus died, he was carried by angels into Abraham's bosom, which was sort of a holding place under the old covenant. The Bible tells us that those who had served God under the old covenant would go to Abraham's bosom and wait for Jesus to complete the work of redemption and lead them to heaven. On the other hand, the rich man died in hell, and the scriptures didn't say anything about angels taking him anywhere.

I believe if Lazarus, who walked upright before God under Old Testament Law, was carried by angels into Abraham's bosom under the old covenant, then surely angels would escort born-again Christians into the throne room of God under the new covenant. Now that's my opinion, and you can take it or leave it. Yet, I believe scripture gives us every reason to believe it's true. "How can we know for sure," somebody asks. I guess we'll just have to wait and see.

Either way, there are angels to watch over us and care for us from the beginning all the way to the end of life, so we might as well get used to them. Isaiah 6 talks about cherubim flying around the throne of God crying, "Holy, holy, holy, holy, holy." So we might as well get used to angels down here, because we're going to keep company with a lot of them in heaven.

But again, angels are not to be worshipped, adored or magnified. God did not send angels down here for us to minister to them; God sent angels down here to minister to us and for us. Heaven is working hand in hand with the Church, and we need to benefit from heaven's help.

No Shortage of Angels

God's Word is clear about the fact that there is definitely no shortage of angels. In fact, think about this. If every child who enters this world has an angel of his or her own, that means we have around 7 billion angels down here on earth to go along with the 7 billion human beings on this earth. Wow—that's a lot of angels. And it's just the beginning.

The book of Revelation talks about great numbers of angels. It says there are 10,000 times 10,000 and then thousands of thousands of angels. I'm not sure how many zeros that would be or what you could do with that on a calculator; mine doesn't have that many zeros. But it's *a lot!*

That's more than enough angels to obey any commission or assignment from God and provide any and all help any believer could ever need from beginning to end.

Your Own Angel

I remember an important revelation the late Kenneth E. Hagin, a well-known and well-respected minister, shared about angels. I've heard Brother Hagin tell many times how Jesus appeared to him in a vision to teach him about the purpose and function of angels. The account is also described in his book, *I Believe in Visions.**

Brother Hagin was kneeling on the platform during a service praying when Jesus appeared to him in a vision to talk about his ministry. Standing behind Jesus was a big, tall fellow whom he later described to be at least seven feet tall or more.

Brother Hagin said Jesus began to talk to him about his sister who had received a serious diagnosis from doctors. Brother Hagin had been praying for his sister just before Jesus appeared. Jesus told him, "Your sister will live and not die. There is no danger of immediate death." Jesus also told Brother Hagin that his sister would live at least another five years, and she did.

Then Brother Hagin said, "Every time I looked at the angel standing behind Jesus, he would look back at me like he wanted to say something." Brother Hagin said he would look at the angel and then look away, thinking to himself, *I've got Jesus here talking to me.* But then Brother Hagin said, "I would look back, and the angel seemed like he wanted to say something again."

Finally, Brother Hagin asked Jesus, "Who is this angel and what does he represent?"

"That's your angel," Jesus said.

"What do you mean *my angel?* Brother Hagin asked.

Jesus quoted Matthew 19:14, "…Suffer little children, and forbid them not, to come unto me: for of such is the kingdom of heaven."

Jesus also quoted the scripture we read earlier in Matthew 18:10 that says an angel is assigned to every child.

Then Jesus said to Brother Hagin, "You don't lose your angel just because you grow up." That's quite a revelation when you think about it. It means whether you appropriate angelic help or not—or whether you recognize angelic help or not—God has assigned an angel to help *you* just the same.

Jesus told Brother Hagin, "The angel has brought a message for you."

"But, Lord, You are here," Brother Hagin said. "Why can't you deliver the message?" Understand that Brother Hagin was not being belligerent or disrespectful; he was just a real stickler for the Word of God, and he didn't want to do anything that could not be founded on scripture.

> IT MEANS WHETHER YOU APPROPRIATE ANGELIC HELP OR NOT—OR WHETHER YOU RECOGNIZE ANGELIC HELP OR NOT—GOD HAS ASSIGNED AN ANGEL TO HELP YOU JUST THE SAME.

Jesus outlined several scriptures for him about angels delivering guidance and messages that we will look at in more detail in Chapter 6. Jesus mentioned an angel breaking Peter out of jail in Acts 12 and an angel giving Philip direction in Acts 8. Jesus pointed out that an angel stood by Paul aboard ship in Acts 27 and gave him direction, and Jesus Himself also appeared to Paul in Acts 22 with comfort and directions. So we see that an angel of the Lord appeared to Paul to give him direction, and Jesus also appeared to Paul with words of comfort and direction.

After hearing Jesus quote these scriptures, Brother Hagin said to the angel, "What is it you have to say to me?" The angel began to share with him about some financial matters Brother Hagin had prayed about and told him how to handle a matter. Brother Hagin said every one of those things came to pass exactly as the angel had said.

You might wonder, *Why did Jesus and an angel both appear to talk to Brother Hagin?* I don't know. God is God, and He can scripturally do whatever He wants to do. We aren't going to figure God out with formulas or calculators or anything else. The only way we'll know God is by His Word. He never goes outside the boundaries of His Word, but He'll do everything within the boundaries of His Word. There's also a mysterious side to God. He's Father, but He is still God. He is Creator of the Universe. He is Almighty God, and He has left Himself room to do things in unusual ways.

Worshipping Angels

Even though we become more and more aware of angels on standby to help us, the Bible specifically talks to us about not worshipping angels or becoming too focused on them. They're not here to be worshipped, and they're not here to entertain us. Angels aren't here to have a cup of coffee with us or play a board game. Angels are not heavenly butlers sent down here to serve us breakfast, pick out our clothes for the day or babysit our kids.

It's not an angel's job to train up a couple's children. The Bible says that parents should train up a child in the way he or she should go. Those are things we as human beings are supposed to do.

In other words, we should do everything we know to do, and God will cause angels to step in to do what we cannot do. God expects us, as His children, to do what we know to do in every situation that comes along. God expects us to walk by faith and walk by wisdom, following the Word of God and the Spirit of God. When we cannot do any more, that's when God will pick up where we leave off and assign angels to step in to supernaturally assist us.

Angels of Power and Might

These powerful angels that step in to help us are the big, powerful, mighty and awesome angels the Bible talks about. Angels are definitely not cupid-like creatures sitting on clouds strumming harps. They're not chubby little babies who wear diapers, float on clouds and shoot bows and arrows.

God's angels we read about throughout the Bible also are not ever portrayed as females in long white flowing gowns like we see in museum paintings or building facades and statues around the world. The angels I'm talking about are the same big, powerful guys the Bible talks about.

It's important to allow the Bible to set our thinking straight on the topic of angels so we'll recognize how mighty and powerful they are and so we don't open up ourselves to counterfeits, (which we'll talk about more in Chapter 8).

Awhile back an angel supposedly showed up to a number of people—ministers included. She was supposed to be very beautiful and about 22 years old. But, friend, that's outside the boundary of the Bible; there's nothing in the Bible like that—not one single time.

> ANGELS ARE DEFINITELY NOT CUPID-LIKE CREATURES SITTING ON CLOUDS STRUMMING HARPS. THEY'RE NOT CHUBBY LITTLE BABIES WHO WEAR DIAPERS, FLOAT ON CLOUDS AND SHOOT BOWS AND ARROWS.

Frankly, the Bible never represents angels as women. I know we can find plenty of female angels on TV, in the movies, on greeting cards and in pictures, but one place they're not found is in the Bible. The Bible says angels are neither male nor female; they are spirit beings. However, the Bible does often represent angels as "male." All the way through the Bible angels are represented as male, though again, in reality they are neither male nor female. Not one time in the Bible are angels ever given the form, shape or appearance of a female. So anytime

I start hearing about female angels showing up—no matter how much good they might do—it doesn't make any difference. It's not Bible; I don't find it in the Scriptures.

Again, we need to understand what God says about angels—what they are and how they work—right straight from the Bible. If we don't speak the Bible truth and tell it right, then God won't be able to manifest angelic help the way He wants to in the days to come and the way we need Him to in the days to come.

We have the Holy Spirit, we have the Word of God, and we need to know the difference between things of God and things that are not of God. The world is messed up enough as it is so we sure don't need the Church adding to its confusion. Let's stay with the Bible. If we do, then I believe God will step up angelic assistance in the earth at every turn.

Chapter Three

ANGELS THROUGH THE BIBLE

Angels can be seen helping the children of God in many different ways from cover to cover throughout the Bible. In the Old Testament, angels dramatically protected God's children and often delivered the nation of Israel during battle. In the New Testament, angels announced the resurrection of Jesus and were on hand for everything from jailbreaks to surviving shipwrecks. As we look at how angels helped God's children through the Bible, it will increase our expectation of how angels can help you and me.

Angels in the Old Testament

Let's look closely at a few Old Testament examples where God's Word describes how angels miraculously assisted God's children.

In 2 Kings 6, we read where God sent angels to rescue the prophet Elisha. The king of Syria came against Israel, setting a trap to kill them. But God empowered Elisha to supernaturally know where the trap had been set, and he warned the king of Israel, saying, "Don't go that way! It's a trap!"

So the Israelites decided to go another way, but the king of Syria only set another trap. Again the prophet of God had inside information and told the king of Israel, "Don't go that direction. There's a trap set for you!"

This happened again and again until finally the king of Syria said, "OK, we've got a traitor here somewhere. Somebody is telling those Israelites where the traps will be set." Finally one of the guys in his camp said, "No, sir. There's no traitor in the camp. There's a man of God over there, who even knows what you whisper in your bedroom. You won't be sneaking up on the Israelites any time soon because God tells that prophet what's going on. Wherever and whenever you set up a trap, God will tell him, and they will go another direction."

The king was furious. "Find that prophet and bring him here!" the Syrian king ordered. Searching high and low, the king's men finally found out that Elisha was in a place called Dothan. So the Syrian king sent "…horses and chariots and a great army there, and they came by night and surrounded the city" (2 Kings 6:14 NKJV).

Maybe you've been in a situation where you feel like there is no way out, and you feel liked you've been chased and backed into a corner. That was the case here. God had been using Elisha mightily to deliver the nation of Israel. But suddenly the whole city was surrounded by a great host of skilled Syrian warriors. These warriors really knew what they were doing, and as far as natural circumstances were concerned, Elisha didn't stand a chance of getting out alive.

Notice the next verse.

> **2 Kings 6:15 (NKJV)**
> And when the servant of the man of God arose early and went out, there was an army, surrounding the city with horses and chariots. And his servant said to him, 'Alas, my master! What shall we do?'

In other words, the servant was saying, "Hey, we're in big trouble!" He looked outdoors and saw a great host, or in plainer language, he saw countless troops of soldiers who didn't look very friendly. It didn't matter what direction he looked; they were completely surrounded. They were in trouble!

"What in the world are we going to do?" the servant asked Elisha.

"Fear not!" Elisha said. Elisha got that advice from God because God always says fear not. God doesn't lead by fear; He delivers *from* fear. Fear is never the voice of God.

Reading on in verse 16, "...[Elisha] answered, 'Do not fear, for those who *are* with us *are* more than those who *are* with them'" (NKJV). They had supernatural back up! God had come to their rescue, and if God can do this for the Israelites under the old covenant, He can sure do it for you and me under the new covenant.

We need to get a hold of the fact that it doesn't matter what dangerous times—situations, circumstances, symptoms, thoughts or attacks—come along in the world or in your life. It doesn't matter what comes against you because those that be with you are a whole lot more than those that be with them.

> IT DOESN'T MATTER WHETHER YOU SEE GOD'S HELP OR NOT, YOU CAN ALWAYS BE CONFIDENT IT'S THERE.

Elisha knew there was no need for the servant to fear. Why? "...'For those who *are* with us *are* more than those who *are* with them.' And Elisha prayed, and said, 'LORD, I pray, open his eyes that he may see...'" (2 Kings 6:16-17 NKJV).

Actually, at first it might not have seemed to be such a good idea for the prophet to pray the servant's eyes be opened. After all, his eyes had been open and that was the problem. He had seen enemy troops with horses and chariots lined up ready to attack and kill them.

Nevertheless, the prophet prayed, "Lord, open his eyes." That tells me that apparently we have more than one set of eyes; we have natural, physical eyes, and we have spiritual eyes. I don't know if the prophet saw the angelic host or not. But obviously whether he saw the angel army or not, he was confident that supernatural help was on site somewhere.

When you think about it, it doesn't matter whether you see God's help or not, you can always be confident it's there. But in this instance, the prophet prayed, "Lord, open his [the servant's] eyes...." He didn't say, "Lord, open *my* eyes." He said, "Lord, open *his* eyes."

Elisha knew the servant just didn't get it, so I'm sure Elisha said to the Lord, "I already know You've got this situation covered, God. But help the boy!" So he prayed the Lord would show the servant.

Notice verse 17 again, paying particular attention to the last phrase.

> **2 Kings 6:17 (NKJV)**
>
> And Elisha prayed, and said, 'Lord, I pray, open his eyes that he may see.' Then the Lord opened the eyes of the young man, and he saw. And behold, the mountain *was* full of horses and chariots of fire all around Elisha.

Did God send chariots of fire around Samaria? No. Were horses and chariots of fire around the servant boy? No. Isn't that interesting? The scripture doesn't say the city was surrounded with God's help. It doesn't say the servant was surrounded with God's help. It said Elisha, the man of God, was surrounded with God's help and great victory came down that day.

One key to the victory was that Elisha knew what to do when he was surrounded, and apparently, it isn't automatic. Elisha knew how to activate the angelic forces of heaven. We can tell by what Elisha said that he was confident the forces of heaven were there on standby to help him and protect him. That's why he asked God to open the eyes of his servant, so he could see angelic help on every side.

Think about what this means to us. If the man of God could activate angels when trouble came his way, then we can too. As a prophet under the old covenant, Elisha was anointed with the Holy Spirit *upon* Him, which equipped him to hear from God and empowered Him to obey God. But we live under a new covenant today, where every born again, Spirit-filled believer now has the same Holy Spirit on the *inside* equipping and empowering him or her. This means that just like Elisha, we can activate angelic help and be victorious over our enemies. (We'll talk more about activating angels in Chapter 10).

Noisy Angels to the Rescue

We find another Old Testament example of angelic protection in 2 Kings 6, where the Syrian army besieged the city of Samaria. Instead of ravaging the city and killing everybody, this time the Syrian army planned to starve them out.

The Syrian army had traveled through the countryside murdering, plundering, killing and robbing. So this conquering army stored up a lot of spoils or goods. Every time they conquered a city, they loaded up with gold, silver, clothes, food and anything good they could haul out of there. In fact, with all the food and water and goods they loaded up, they could last on the outskirts of Samaria indefinitely.

Unfortunately inside the city, things got really bad. There was very little food on the inside, and of course, the city was surrounded so the people couldn't go beyond the city walls to get food. What little food that existed was sold for an extremely high dollar, and even it was running out. The Bible talks about one horrific case where a woman was so hungry she boiled her own child and ate him. How shocking is that? I don't think it could get worse than people starving and eating their children. Life in the city was wild and desperate.

When the king heard what was going on, he hollered out, "Cut Elisha's head off his shoulders by tomorrow!" The people were starving, and as a result he was mad at the prophet and sent his army to capture him.

Meanwhile, Elisha was sitting with the elders of Israel in his house when the King of Israel's messenger showed up to capture him. The prophet told him, "Now listen. Here's the word of the Lord. By tomorrow at this time, you will be able to get anything you want. You will be able to get food for pennies on the dollar. You'll have a flood of supply coming in."

One of the king's right hand men heard that and said, "If only there were windows in heaven. I mean how could we go from starvation to abundance in 24 hours? Even if there were windows in heaven, it couldn't improve that much."

The problem with that guy was that he didn't realize that heaven does have some big windows. In fact, the Bible says in Genesis 7 that God opened them up, and it rained 40 days and 40 nights flooding the entire earth. In Malachi 3 God even said, "Anytime I can find a tither, I'll open up the windows again. Instead of pouring water, I'll pour out a blessing." So don't ever forget that God has open windows, even if the king's assistant didn't realize it.

How did the prophet answer the king's assistant? He said, "Because you don't believe, you'll see it, but you won't be able to partake of it."

While all this was happening with the city under siege and people starving, four lepers unclean by Levitical law sat outside by the city gate. By law they should not even have been in public, let alone enter the city. The Bible said they lay outside the gate reasoning together or talking about something. I don't think it's too hard to figure out that they probably were talking about how hungry they were.

I imagine their conversation went like this: "We're trapped for sure. If we go into this city, we would starve because they don't have any food. Or if we go over to the Syrian camp, they might give us something to eat, but then they would kill us. Either way, we're dead."

Finally the four lepers decided that going to the Syrian camp was a better idea, so they hiked on over to see if somebody would throw them a morsel of food. But they approached the Syrian camp only to discover the place was empty. There was gold. There was silver. There was clothing. There was food. But there were no people.

What happened? We read in 2 Kings 7 that as the four lepers began hiking their way over to the Syrian camp, God caused the enemy army to hear horses and chariots and a great army host. Imagine that! God caused four lepers to sound like three huge armies. When the Syrian camp heard the horses and chariots, they panicked, saying, "The king's hired another army. He's hired the Egyptians, and they're coming to get us." It scared the Syrian camp so badly they ran for their lives. They left so fast they didn't bother to pack a single item and left all their valuables behind.

I don't know about you, but I've thought a lot about the angelic army the enemy heard. I've wondered, *What could make that kind of noise where four lepers sounded like a huge host of horses and chariots?* It sounds to me like an angelic army was dispatched from heaven in great force, and God opened up the Syrian ears to hear it.

With the Syrian camp deserted, the lepers filled their pockets up with gold and silver. They tried on all the clothes they wanted and collected things to bury. Then they started all over again gathering up more. They filled their pockets again with gold and silver and ate all the food they could eat. Then they did it again, and hid and buried more, saying, "If the folks in Samaria catch us, we'll be in real trouble."

> AN ANGELIC ARMY WAS DISPATCHED FROM HEAVEN IN GREAT FORCE, AND GOD OPENED UP THE SYRIAN EARS TO HEAR IT.

Finally the lepers told the folks in Samaria that the enemy camp was empty, and the Samarians stampeded the camp and collected all the rest of the spoils. The king's servant who didn't believe the Word of the Lord was caught in the stampede and crushed.

By the next day, a person could buy anything at any price—pennies on the dollar, just as the prophet of God had said. There was a great abundance of food because God had taken the wealth of the sinner and brought it into the hands of the just. God has a way of doing that.

How did God deliver an entire city of people about to starve to death? It looks to me like He sent an angelic army to get the job done.

A Sound in the Mulberry Trees

We find another Old Testament example of angelic help in 1 Chronicles 14. It tells of King David who drove the Philistines off God's territory. Let's read verses 9-10, 12.

> **1 Chronicles 14:9-10, 12**
>
> 9 And the Philistines came and spread themselves in the valley of Rephaim.
>
> 10 And David enquired of God, saying, Shall I go up against the Philistines? And wilt thou deliver them into mine hand? And the Lord said unto him, Go up; for I will deliver them into thine hand.
>
> 12 And when they had left their gods there, David gave a commandment, and they were burned with fire.

Essentially David asked God, "What in the world are we going to do about these Philistines?"

"Go, and I'll deliver them into your hands," God answered.

David did just as God had said, and God drove the enemy out. David destroyed and burned every one of their false gods.

Then again, those Philistines weren't the sharpest knives in the drawer, so it wasn't long before they tried it again and returned to the camp in the same valley. Once again David asked God what to do. Verse 14 says David enquired of God, and God said to him, "Don't go up after them!"

This is a great Bible example of how important it is to be led by the Spirit of God—then and now. One of the most important lessons a Christian can learn is how to be led by the Spirit. We cannot afford to get into a rut where we think, *A certain plan worked last time, so I'll just do it again this time.* Getting in a rut will get you in a big mess..

To obtain God's supernatural help and to activate angelic help in any situation, we must be led by the Holy Spirit. Notice how King David handled things. He didn't just charge into battle like a bull in a glass shop, saying, "Man, we'll whip them!" No. He said, "God, what do we do?"

We all need to ask that question on a regular basis. We would be in much better shape if we would say, "God, what do I do in this situation? Is this the right way to go? Is there a better way to go? Is there a better way to handle this situation?"

"Wait! How could King David, who lived under the old covenant, be led by the Spirit of God?" somebody asks. Of course, King David was not born again, but he was anointed with the Spirit of God *upon* him. As we mentioned earlier, today under a new and better covenant, a born-again person can have the Spirit of God *within* his or her spirit or inner person. Thank God that today a person doesn't have to be a king or a prophet to be led by the Holy Spirit. Every born again Christian can be led in the inner "man" or person of the heart by the Spirit of God.

But in 1 Chronicles 14:14, "David enquired again of God; and God said unto him, Go not up after them; turn away from them, and come upon them over against the mulberry trees." In essence, God told David that instead of going after them, he should turn and run or fake them out, as we might say today.

Now notice the next few verses.

1 Chronicles 14:15-17

15 And it shall be, when thou shalt hear *a sound of going in the tops of the mulberry trees,* that then thou shalt go out to battle: for God is gone forth before thee to smite the host of the Philistines.

16 David therefore did as God commanded him: and they smote the host of the Philistines from Gibeon even to Gazer.

17 And the fame of David went out into all lands; and the Lord brought the fear of him upon all nations.

That must have been some battle. Someday I'd like to watch that battle play out in the video room of heaven.

Look again at what it said in verse 15, "It shall be, when thou shalt hear a sound of going in the tops of the mulberry trees...." *A sound in the mulberry trees?* If God Himself hadn't said that, we might have to wonder what mulberry trees could possibly have to do with anything.

I still vaguely recall a song about mulberry trees that was sung in a Pentecostal church where I got filled with the Holy Spirit as a young man. It went something like this, *"I can hear the rustling in the mulberry trees, and I know, I know, I know the move is on."* I wondered even then what in the world that meant. But one day I read about the mulberry trees in the Bible and realized those mulberry trees make a pretty important point.

The way the King James translation phrases 1 Chronicles 14:15 isn't really clear, so let me read verse 15 from a couple of other translations. The Amplified Bible says, "When you hear a sound of marching in the tops of the mulberry trees or balsam trees...." The Message Bible says, "When you hear a sound like shuffling feet in the tops of the balsams...." The Bible in Basic English says, "And at the sound of footsteps in the tops of the trees, go out to the fight, for God has gone out before you to overcome the army of the Philistines."

> WHEN THEY HEARD FOOTSTEPS IN THE TREE TOPS MARCHING, THEY WERE HEARING THE ANGEL ARMY OF GOD COMING TO DO BATTLE FOR THE CHILDREN OF GOD.

Who do you suppose was walking or making noise at tree-top level?

Let me read you one more translation. When the Bible was translated, the Old Testament was translated into the Aramaic, and here's what the translators said of verse 15, "When thou shall hear the sound of the angels coming to thy assistance, then go out to battle for an angel is sent from the presence of God that He may render thy way prosperous."

So what made the sound up in the mulberry trees? *Angels!* Those were angels walking about tree height. When King David and his army heard "a sound of going" in the treetops, when they heard the sound of shuffling, when they heard footsteps in the tree tops marching up there, they were hearing the angel army of God coming to do battle for the children of God.

God had said, "...When you hear a sound of marching in the tops of the mulberry trees, then go to battle for I've gone before you." How was God able to go ahead of them? God sent His angels out ahead, and they overcame the Philistines and brought great deliverance to David and his army. All through the Old Testament, we see where God delivered His children with the power of angelic forces.

Angels in the New Testament

Angels are just as apparent in the New Testament as they were in the Old Testament. Angels announced Jesus' birth, His ministry and His resurrection. And Jesus will come back in great glory with angels announcing His return. The book of Revelation tells us more about the end of the age than any other book, and it is filled with angelic activity from beginning to end.

When Jesus was born, the angel appeared to the shepherds watching over their flocks by night. Let's read what happens next.

> **Luke 2:9-14 (NKJV)**
>
> 9 And behold, an angel of the Lord stood before them, and the glory of the Lord shone around them, and they were greatly afraid.
>
> 10 Then the angel said to them, "Do not be afraid, for behold, I bring you good tidings of great joy which will be to all people.
>
> 11 "for there is born to you this day in the city of David a Savior, who is Christ the Lord.
>
> 12 "And this will be the sign to you: You will find a Babe wrapped in swaddling cloths, lying in a manger."
>
> 13 And suddenly there was with the angel a multitude of the heavenly host praising God and saying:
>
> 14 "Glory to God in the highest, And on earth peace, goodwill toward men!"

When Jesus was in the wilderness being tempted by the devil and fasting 40 days and 40 nights, the Bible says afterward He was ministered to by angels (Matthew 4).

Angels were also on the scene when Jesus was raised from the dead. When loved ones went to the tomb to finish the embalming process, they saw an angel. Mark 16 tells us the story.

> **Mark 16:2-6 (NKJV)**
> 2 Very early in the morning, on the first day of the week, they came to the tomb when the sun had risen.
> 3 And they said among themselves, "Who will roll away the stone from the door of the tomb for us?"
> 4 But when they looked up, they saw that the stone had been rolled away—for it was very large.
> 5 And entering the tomb, they saw a young man clothed in a long white robe sitting on the right side; and they were alarmed.
> 6 But he said to them, "Do not be alarmed. You seek Jesus of Nazareth, who was crucified. He is risen! He is not here. See the place where they laid Him."

These scriptures and many more prove there's no limit to the help angels provided to believers throughout the New Testament, and there's no limit to the help they will provide believers today.

Supernatural Jailbreak

In Acts 12 we read that Peter was next in line to be killed, so an angel showed up to break him out of prison. Herod had already proven he was capable of great cruelty by killing James with a sword. When he saw it pleased the people, he threw Peter in jail and figured that would make the Jews even happier. Herod was not what you would call a really merciful guy.

The minute the early church heard this news they got busy praying. In fact, the margin of my Bible says the church went to *"instant and earnest prayer"* (Acts 12:5). I can imagine what the early Christians were thinking, *We've already lost James, so we're sure not going to lose Peter, too. We lost James because we didn't do anything, so let's get busy and stop this now.*

About the time the church was earnestly praying, Peter had been confined to prison and was on the floor asleep between two soldiers. Keep in mind that it wasn't a prison like we hear about today. They didn't have bathrooms, showers, weight rooms, television sets, libraries, laundry facilities or even a cafeteria. Back in those days the prison was dark and damp and not at all a nice place.

Peter faced what seemed like a hopeless situation. Have you ever felt like you landed in one of those? Really, the truth is that situations are anything but hopeless because God is greater than all that. God is greater than what Peter faced, and He's greater than whatever you face.

Sure, Peter was put in prison by a murderous king about to take his head off. Sure, the doors were locked, and Peter had no way out. Not only were there soldiers outside the door, but also Peter slept on the floor in chains with a Roman soldier on each side of him. Those soldiers were stationed there with the sole purpose of making sure Peter never got out of the place. But suddenly! Here it comes! A bright light shined into the prison. Help had come!

> PETER WAS PROBABLY SNORING AWAY WHILE THE BIG OLD ANGEL HAD TO NUDGE HIM, SAYING, "GET UP, PETER! GET YOUR COAT ON! GET YOUR SHOES ON! LET'S GET OUT OF HERE!"

Peter was so sound asleep that he didn't even open an eye. Man, talk about somebody at peace and at rest in a hopeless situation. Peter was probably snoring away while the big old angel had to nudge him, saying, "Get up, Peter! Get your coat on! Get your shoes on! Let's get out of here!" Think about it. Peter was so sound asleep the angel had to kick him to wake him up.

It appeared that not a single soldier woke up—not the ones outside and not the ones inside. But the chains fell off Peter, and he walked right on out the door with the angel.

That's some supernatural account. Peter was about to lose his life, but an angel walked in and the chains fell off. The door swung open, and Peter and the angel walked to the nearby courtyard. The angel disappeared, and before you know it, Peter was on his way to church.

Meanwhile, we know the church members were still in instant and earnest prayer because they didn't answer the door when Peter knocked. Peter had walked across town and knocked on the church door, but the church members were so busy praying they didn't even answer the knock. I doubt Peter tapped gently either, but still the church members were too busy and too focused on God to hear or bother with someone banging on the door. They were determined to pray until God delivered Peter, and God had delivered Peter through the avenue of an angel leading a supernatural jailbreak.

If the Church today would learn that same tenacity in prayer, I believe we would experience more results, lose fewer ministry gifts and witness many more miracles. If we would learn tenacity of prayer—learn to stay with whatever we're praying about with bulldog tenacity—we would see greater victories.

Listen to me now. The prayer of faith in Mark 11:24 will not obtain every answer we need. But it is absolutely the right prayer for an *individual* to pray because it says what things soever **you** desire when **you** pray, believe **you** receive them, and **you will** have them. But when you are praying for somebody else, sometimes it requires a fervent, continued, stick-with-it-until-the-answer-comes kind of prayer.

There's something about corporate or united prayer that really gets the job done when nothing else works. The early church had gotten a hold of that principle, and God responded with an angel to set Peter free.

Chapter Four

God's Enforcers of Protection

God never promised we wouldn't face problems in life or walk through hard times. He did not promise that life would always be rosy, but God did give us His Word to teach us how to live victoriously. God's plan is for us to be more than conquerors living in abundance in every area of life, and that's what God has always wanted for His children. God proves it with thousands and thousands of Bible promises and then enforces His Word with angelic back up.

Psalm 91 is one of those promises of protection. Actually, some Bible scholars believe God gave Psalm 91 to Moses as the Israelites crossed the Red Sea and headed into dangerous territory on their way to the Promised Land.

Interestingly enough, this particular supernatural insurance policy didn't wait to pay up when the Israelites had problems, and it doesn't wait to pay up when we have problems. It's God's plan to keep His children out of danger altogether. (More detailed teaching about Psalm 91 is available in a book by Mark Brazee titled *Fear-Free Living in Dangerous Times*).

But let me ask, did God want His children to experience 40 years of wilderness? *No!* God wanted His children to live in the Promised Land of plenty, but God couldn't change what His children had chosen for themselves because He gave them the right to choose. God knew His promises in the 91st Psalm—along with God's angelic enforcers—could keep His children safe from anything, anytime, anywhere.

Again, Psalm 91 does not tell us, "Thou shalt cruise through life on a bed of roses and everything will be wonderful with never a challenge, never a problem." That might have been nice in a perfect world before Adam's fall, but as a result of Adam's disobedience we can pretty much expect the devil to raise his ugly head and try to cause trouble for us while we live on this earth. Actually, we can count on it.

> GOD KNEW HIS PROMISES IN THE 91ST PSALM—ALONG WITH GOD'S ANGELIC ENFORCERS—COULD KEEP HIS CHILDREN SAFE FROM ANYTHING, ANYTIME, ANYWHERE.

But Almighty God sent Jesus to restore to us what Adam's treason cost mankind, and God promised throughout His Word to guarantee our protection, safety, defense, healing and health and long life. He's also promised that if we holdfast to the promises of God, we can triumph over the devil in every circumstance.

God's Word isn't just a storybook, and Psalm 91 isn't just a nice poem. God's Word is *alive* and *full of power* because all scripture is given by inspiration of God. Even more to the point here, God wraps up this supernatural insurance policy by pointing out that He's assigned angels to enforce its provisions.

Angelic Enforcers

Let's focus on two verses of Psalm 91, where God points out that He's assigned angels—or we could call them supernatural adjusters—down here on earth to enforce Psalm 91. He's telling us, "I've got special agents and enforcers assigned to your case. They're supernatural insurance adjusters who will adjust whatever needs to be adjusted for you. They will enforce your protection policy."

Notice the kind of heavy duty back up God has promised us in these two verses.

> **Psalm 91:11-12 (NKJV)**
> 11 For He shall give His angels charge over you, To keep you in all your ways.
> 12 In *their* hands they shall bear you up, Lest you dash your foot against a stone.

Verse 11 says that God has given these angels charge over you. Or, in other words, He's assigned angels to guard and protect you. Then verse 12 says, "In their hands they shall bear you up." Those are some mighty huge angels if they're big enough to hold an adult in their *hands*. In fact, these angelic enforcers do a lot more than hold you up; they're assigned to watch over you and take care of you.

These verses remind me of how parents sometimes ask older siblings to keep an eye on younger kids when the parents are gone from the house. A parent might say to an older child, "I'm leaving you in charge." What does the parent expect? The parent expects that even if the older child remains in the background, he or she better know what's going on and be alert. If trouble shows up, the parent expects the older child to protect the family and *take charge*.

Aren't you glad to know that your heavenly Father has given your angel the same kind of assignment? He expects *your angel* to guard and protect *you*, defend *you*, watch out for *you* and take care of *you*.

'You're in Charge!'

Let me give you another example. When I was about 15 years old, I worked for a guy during the summertime laying sod at new apartment complexes. Three of us worked all morning, and then we'd jump in a truck and all head to lunch together. We would always find a restaurant with a buffet, and I can tell you the restaurant didn't make any money on the three of us the way we ate.

Our boss drove the truck to lunch each day, and I still remember how he had a big book filled with all of his contacts and paperwork. Sometimes he even had wads of cash hanging out of the thing. Other times he would put an old rubber band around a big wad of cash and throw the whole stack on the front dashboard of his truck as we headed into the restaurant. It was so hot in the summer that the truck windows were usually rolled down even though that big wad of cash sat in plain sight on the dashboard.

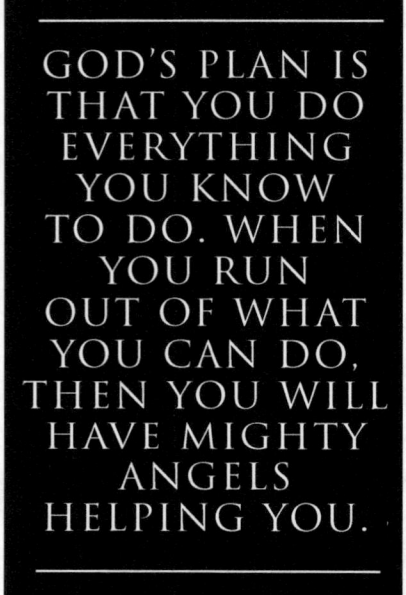

GOD'S PLAN IS THAT YOU DO EVERYTHING YOU KNOW TO DO. WHEN YOU RUN OUT OF WHAT YOU CAN DO, THEN YOU WILL HAVE MIGHTY ANGELS HELPING YOU.

The guy never worried even once that all that money would be stolen. Do you know why?

His dog waited in the truck.

The dog was really friendly and always rode around in the truck with us. But when we would go into the restaurant, the boss would say to the dog, "You're in charge!"

Early on I remember thinking, *I hope the guy knows what he's doing. Anybody could reach in and grab that roll of money.*

But one time I watched as somebody innocently walked past the truck, and the dog came really close to taking a bite out of the person. That dog knew he was in charge, and after that we did, too. On an average day, that dog was friendly—even lazy—until somebody looked at the roll of cash. Then that old dog took charge really quick.

Thank God, we don't have to be concerned about lazy angels. It may not seem like they're doing much sometimes, but when something tries to cause trouble for the person they're assigned to watch, then all of a sudden they *take charge*.

"How come angels aren't doing something all the time?" somebody might ask. They don't need to do something all the time. God's plan is that you do everything you know to do. When you run out of what you can do, then you will have mighty angels helping you.

Your angel will work when he needs to work. He's not going to tie your shoes, pick out your clothes or serve you lunch. God didn't assign him to do those things. But you've got an angel backing you up, and when you need him, he's there. If you need more than one angel, you get more. You have one assigned for sure, but there are a whole lot more angels on standby when you need help.

Angel Blocks Stabbing

A pastor friend tells the story of how an angel saved the life of his great grandfather, who was one of the pioneers of the Pentecostal movement around the turn of the century. Keep in mind that his grandfather pioneered Pentecostal churches when Pentecost was not popular.

Actually, the Pentecostal message was received so badly back then, there were folks who would burn down evangelistic tents where the meetings were conducted. But that didn't stop my pastor friend's grandfather. He traveled and set up his tent to preach the Pentecostal message, and God was with him.

My friend shared about one tent meeting in particular when an angry man walked into his grandfather's service. Toward the end of a meeting, the man walked into the back of the tent and called out to the grandfather preaching on the platform. Loudly and harshly the man said, "I want to talk to you outside!"

"Sure," the grandfather answered the man. Then the Lord spoke in the grandfather's heart and said to him, "But don't yield to fear or the man will kill you."

The grandfather walked back through the tent with the man and went outside with him. "All of the sudden," the grandfather said, "I looked down and the guy had a huge dagger up the sleeve of his coat. He pulled it out and lifted it up. I couldn't even flinch. I just stood there."

The man thrust the dagger down to stab the grandfather, but as the knife got about six inches from stabbing him, the knife was blocked. It stopped like it had hit a wall or something. The man tried five times to stab the grandfather, but the fifth time the man turned, jumped over the bushes and took off running.

The Lord spoke to the grandfather and said, "Don't tell anybody what happened." So he returned to the tent meeting and continued preaching the service like nothing had happened.

Several nights later, a guy showed up at the altar and prayed almost all night long. By morning the man got born again and filled with the Holy Spirit.

> WHAT DO YOU THINK BLOCKED THE GUY'S KNIFE? I BELIEVE HE BUMPED INTO ONE OF GOD'S ENFORCERS OF THE 91ST PSALM.

Then the grandfather shared, "I got to baptize him in water the next night. As I was baptizing him, he shared his testimony and said, 'I'm the one who tried to stab you. But I could not get the knife in you because I kept running into something that stopped it.'"

"I had never believed in God or religion," the man continued, "but I couldn't stab you because I ran into something big and real protecting you. Suddenly I believed in God and religion. I decided right then and there that I had to get God in my life, so I got born again and baptized in the Holy Spirit."

What do you think blocked the guy's knife? I believe He bumped into one of God's enforcers of the 91st Psalm.

Angels Join the Football Team

I heard a story years ago of an angel rescuing two girls walking home from a meeting on the outskirts of a college campus late one night. As they walked along, they heard something behind them. It was very dark, but they were able to see some shady looking characters following them so they picked up their pace.

When they came to the next street light, they looked back again and saw that the guys were a little closer. So they hurried even faster. By the time they got to the next street light, they looked back again and realized the guys were really gaining on them. The two young co-eds were really scared and knew they were in trouble. The girls prayed earnestly.

Pretty soon they came to the next street light, and this time they looked back and saw three or four members of their college football team with their jerseys on. They were massive guys that blocked the view between the girls and the bad guys, and the girls were so unbelievably relieved.

"Thank you, Jesus! Thank You! Thank You! Thank You that You've called out the football team to protect us!" the girls called out. Best yet, while the girls shouted praises, they realized that when the bad guys saw the football team, they took off running in the other direction.

Yet as the girls walked a little further excitedly talking about what God had done for them, they stopped and stared at each other in shock. "Wait a minute," they said out loud at the same time. "Our school doesn't have a football team!"

Do you think their school got a new football team just in time? No. Were they imagining things? No. I believe God sent an angelic team to their rescue.

We could go on and on with stories like this because God is not a respecter of persons. What He's done for many, He'll do for you. God will watch over you. He'll take care of you. He'll bless you. He'll prosper you and with long life He'll satisfy you. His angels will pick you up and carry you in their hands. That's right! They will pick you up in the palm of their hands because they're big angels with lots of experience, they've been around for ages and generations, and they have lots of practice taking care of folks.

Quote Psalm 91 over yourself and your loved ones often, saying: "I'm dwelling in the secret place of the most high. I say of the Lord, He's my refuge. He's my fortress. He's my God in Him I'll put my trust. No evil shall overtake me. No plague shall come near my dwelling. And God has given His angels charge over me to watch over me, protect me and help me."

Angels Halt Mexican Mafia

We received an email awhile back from missionaries out of our church in Mexico who shared how angels supernaturally protected them on the field. You've probably heard news reports about the turbulent drug wars in Mexico between drug lords and the Mexican mafia. Headlines have reported violent shootings and murders, and our missionaries emailed to say activity had escalated to an all-time high in their region of Mexico.

As a matter of fact, three of our DOMATA School of Ministry graduates, two pastors and one of the youth, were eating in a restaurant in Mexico when for no apparent reason the mafia walked in armed with semi-automatics and killed 10 people. Praise God, our grads were unharmed as they lay on the floor claiming the 91st Psalm. God's Word works! It doesn't matter how bad the world is or how bad the world becomes, God is always faithful to honor His Word. As our grads put their trust in God's Word, God sent angels to shield and deflect bullets for them.

Angelic Safety Squad

A few years ago Janet and I met a couple for the first time who shared an interesting report with us about God's protection for us. The husband was a pastor, and his wife was a woman given to prayer. We had heard of them, and we had heard about the amazing prayer life of the wife in particular. As we rode along in a car with them on the way to a church service, the wife turned around to us and said, "I've been praying for you and Janet for many years."

I thought to myself, *We've never met this woman before, but thank God for the Holy Ghost leading in prayer.* I was really glad to hear that God had her praying for us, but I was surprised because after all we had never even met before.

She began to talk about the things God had instructed her to pray for us, and she knew more about what we were doing than we knew ourselves. She talked about nations where we had traveled, our missions outreaches and God's leading in our lives.

Keep in mind that we had this conversation back when planes were being hijacked in Europe in the 1980s. Terrorists shot up the Athens, Greece, airport at one point, and we had left the country only weeks before. Planes were being hijacked over Paris, and for awhile people were being shot on the tarmac in Paris.

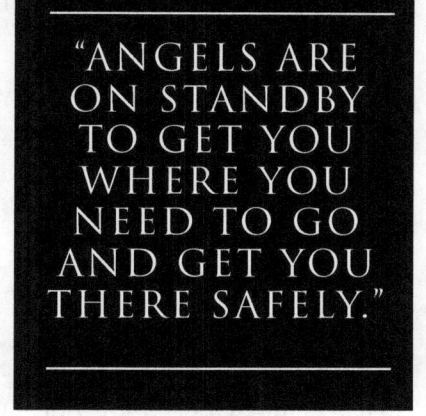

"ANGELS ARE ON STANDBY TO GET YOU WHERE YOU NEED TO GO AND GET YOU THERE SAFELY."

Wouldn't you know just about the time all this shooting was taking place near the Paris airport is about the time God dealt with us to begin traveling to Paris. A lot of our friends and family were saying, "Please don't go over there! You need to pray about it!" Well, we already had prayed about it, and that's why we were going.

"Yeah, but, it's dangerous over there," people would say. The truth is that we're safer over there in the will of God than we are over here in America out of the will of God.

The pastor's wife continued talking and said, "I just want you to know that every time you get on a plane, a team of angels has already boarded and checked out the whole plane. Angels check it out for bombs. Angels check it out for mechanical problems. Angels are on standby to get you where you need to go and get you there safely."

Protection in the Sky

It wasn't long before we had another opportunity to recognize a team of angels working to keep us safe. I remember one time we were leaving Nairobi, Kenya, traveling across Africa. We had flown out of Nairobi, but stopped about four times across Africa until we finally hit Senegal, our last stop. We were on a PanAm 747 jetliner that had picked people up along the way, so by the time we left Dakar it was packed full.

After boarding the plane, we sat on the tarmac until time to leave. As I looked out the window, a particular engine caught my attention. Even though a 747 has four engines, somehow I noticed one engine just didn't seem right. Still, I had a peace on the inside and an urge in my spirit witnessing to me, *Go ahead and go; it's OK.*

As we rolled down the runway and became airborne a little above pattern altitude, the 747 jerked sharply. Then we began to circle and circle and circle. Eventually the pilot announced, "As we were taking off one of our engines blew up, so we've had to drain off fuel so we can land. We're returning to the airport where we'll figure out what to do."

We landed again in Dakar, where they explained an engine was being strapped to another plane and would be flown from London to Dakar while we waited it out. The airline picked up the tab for us to stay at an all-inclusive resort, where we suddenly found ourselves enjoying a great hotel room, long lines of buffet food, swimming pools and beaches. We spent about 24 hours at a luxury resort while mechanics worked on the engine. *There's nothing like getting treated in grand and glorious style,* I thought.

The truth is that even when I felt the plane jerk—a pretty major jerk—I wasn't a bit concerned. Why? Because I knew my angels had already checked out the plane. I knew there was an angel on the left wing, an angel on the right wing, an angel on the nose, an angel on the tail, and I knew our plane was going where it needed to go one way or another. The plane wasn't going down while we were on it. Hallelujah!

Angels Ride the Wings

Recently I read about some guys aboard a plane that was badly shot up in battle during World War II. The plane was so heavily damaged that it didn't look like it could even fly. But one of the guys looked out of the window and saw a huge angel on one wing. He quickly looked out the opposite window and saw another huge angel on the other wing.

With an angel escort, the airplane so badly shot up it didn't look like it could even get airborne flew all the way to the airport and landed safely. When folks looked at that plane, they were shocked and amazed because they said there's no way a plane shot up so badly could fly. But it flew. And it landed.

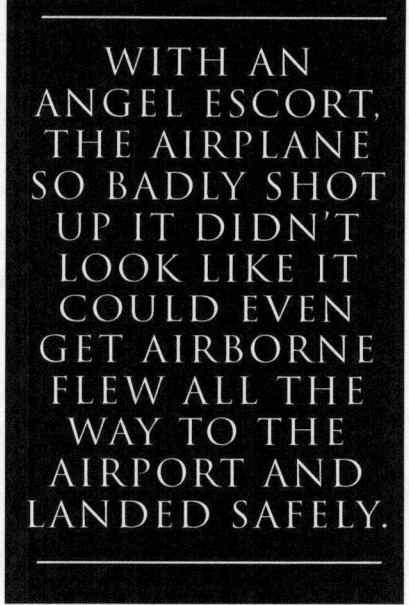

WITH AN ANGEL ESCORT, THE AIRPLANE SO BADLY SHOT UP IT DIDN'T LOOK LIKE IT COULD EVEN GET AIRBORNE FLEW ALL THE WAY TO THE AIRPORT AND LANDED SAFELY.

I tell you what, God is in the protection business. He's in the healing business. He's in the comforting business. He's in the delivering business. God is in the business of sending angels whenever His children need help. If you will believe God's promises of protection—or any of the promises of God's Word—God's angels will enforce the Word from beginning to end in your life.

Chapter Five

Angels Deliver Healings and Miracles

From Adam and Eve to you and me, there's really never been a time when supernatural healings and miracles have not occurred on earth to some degree. But I believe what's transpired up to now is nothing compared to what we're about to see in the days to come. I believe we're about to step into a realm of healings and miracles beyond anything we've ever seen.

We're going to see bodies restored and repaired, and we're going to see amazing creative miracles. Diseases that cannot be fixed by medical science will be fixed by healings and miracles because where medical science leaves off, heaven picks up.

Jesus Himself said greater works are coming, and these greater works will include a great increase in angels delivering healings and miracles. Angels will be working with heaven and with us delivering the greatest outpouring known to man.

Come and See

In John 1 Jesus talked about the greater works to come.

John 1:46-51 (NKJV)
46 And Nathanael said to him, "Can anything good come out of Nazareth?"

> Philip said to him, "Come and see."
>
> 47 Jesus saw Nathanael coming toward Him, and said of him, "Behold, an Israelite indeed, in whom is no deceit!"
>
> 48 Nathanael said to Him, "How do You know me?" Jesus answered and said to him, "Before Philip called you, when you were under the fig tree, I saw you."
>
> 49 Nathanael answered and said to Him, "Rabbi, You are the Son of God! You are the King of Israel!"
>
> 50 Jesus answered and said to him, "Because I said to you, 'I saw you under the fig tree,' do you believe? You will see greater things than these."
>
> 51 And He said to him, "Most assuredly, I say to you, hereafter you shall see heaven open, and the angels of God ascending and descending upon the Son of Man."

It's clear from this passage that Nathanael did not believe Jesus was the Son of God until Jesus suddenly changed his mind. Jesus operated in a word of knowledge that got Nathanael's attention and made a believer out of him.

"When you were sitting under the tree, I saw you," Jesus said to him. Nathanael was impressed.

But Jesus responded, "You're excited because you've seen the supernatural operate—a revelation gift or the word of knowledge. But just wait! You'll see much greater than that."

What is greater than the revelation gifts? The power gifts are greater. The nine gifts of the Spirit listed in 1 Corinthians 12 are often categorized as follows: *revelation gifts* – word of knowledge, word of wisdom, discerning of spirits; *power gifts* – special faith, gifts of healings, working of miracles; *vocal gifts* – divers tongues, interpretation and prophecy.

So, in other words, Jesus was saying to Nathanael, "You were wowed by word of knowledge, but just wait until you see the power gifts of special faith, working of miracles and gifts of healings in operation.

Then look at the important explanation Jesus gave Nathanael and all of us. Jesus said, "...Verily, verily, I say unto you, Hereafter ye shall see heaven open, and *the angels of God ascending and descending upon the Son of man"* (verse 51). Obviously Jesus is saying that angels will be involved in these greater works.

But what would angels have to do with power gifts or special faith, working of miracles and gifts of healings? Angels don't heal people; they're messengers. And why would angels go up and come back down? What would angels go get from the throne of God and bring back to earth that's even greater than the revelation gifts?

I believe angels will bring healings and miracles from heaven to earth. They will bring new lungs, new kidneys, new livers, new hearts, new eyes and any other new body parts that are needed. I believe God has entire warehouses full of body parts in heaven that He wants angels to deliver to His children on earth. Heaven is filled with miracles—miracles needed down here on earth.

I haven't been to heaven, and I don't have scripture to prove there are warehouses there of body parts, but I believe it's true. Henry Ford wasn't the only one with a better idea, and he wasn't the only one with the idea of using spare parts. God designed these human bodies, and He can sure put in a new part from time to time. God can send an angel to deliver healings and miracles anytime He wants.

Pool of Bethesda

In John 5 we read about angels involved with healing at the pool of Bethesda, which was sort of an ancient hospital. History tells us that a wealthy man built the porches or sheds to keep the sick people out of the sun. Yet, there was no physical or medical treatment there and nobody was getting any better.

Let's begin reading in verse two.

> **John 5:2-4**
>
> 2 Now there is at Jerusalem by the sheep market a pool, which is called in the Hebrew tongue Bethesda, having five porches.
>
> 3 In these lay a great multitude of impotent folk, of blind, halt, withered, waiting for the moving of the water.

4 For an angel went down at a certain season into the pool, and troubled the water: whosoever then first after the troubling of the water stepped in was made whole of whatsoever disease he had.

> **WE MIGHT AS WELL GET USED TO ANGELS DELIVERING HEALINGS BECAUSE I BELIEVE WE'RE ABOUT TO SEE A WHOLE LOT MORE OF THEM.**

We read that a great multitude of impotent or sick folk—blind, halt and withered—lay on the porches day after day. That's a lot of sick people. Actually, a multitude was probably about 1,000 people back then, so imagine how many a *great* multitude would be.

You can imagine the people were all wondering when the angel would trouble the waters because the first one in to the water when it was troubled or moved would be healed. It was worth the wait to a sick person because it didn't matter what the ailment was or how long the person had suffered. It didn't matter what the diagnosis or the prognosis was, the first person in the water got healed. Unfortunately, nobody knew when an angel would trouble the water.

But notice that the angel wasn't doing the healing; the angel *brought* the healing from God and deposited it in the pool. Again, angels are not healers; they're messengers. They are delivery "men."

Think about how it works when you order a pizza from a pizza place. The delivery guy doesn't show up and say, "I just cooked this in my car. Here you go." No. He picked up the pizza that was prepared and cooked somewhere else, and he simply delivered it to you. It's the same with angels. They don't heal people. They don't produce the healing; they don't purchase the healing. Jesus provided that Himself when He hung on the cross. But angels can deliver healings, and that's one way God delivers them to you and me.

I believe before we Christians check out at the Rapture, we will see a great and powerful wave of healing flowing through our churches and our cities. We might as well get used to angels delivering healings because I believe we're about to see a whole lot more of them.

Angel Works Healing Crusades

During the Healing Revival from 1947 to 1958, a man named William Branham stood at the forefront of the prophet's ministry and was said to have an angel working with him in the healing ministry. Those familiar with his ministry said the angel played a major role in delivering the healings that occurred in his services and crusades.

"But is it true that he got off into doctrinal error toward the end of his ministry?" somebody might ask. Yes he did, but that shouldn't negate or toss out all the wonderful things he demonstrated before he got off into error. We should learn what we can from him and leave the rest alone.

From everything I've read, Brother Branham was a really shy person. I read that earlier in his life he wanted to be a forest ranger and spent much of his time in the woods enjoying the quiet. That may help to explain why those familiar with his ministry describe him as very uncomfortable in a crowd of people and timid, almost like a "scared rabbit."

Yet, thousands of people showed up for his meetings. Interestingly enough, people say Brother Branham was usually jittery and nervous until the angel who worked with him in the healing ministry showed up in the room. I don't know of his meetings firsthand, but folks have said when he would see the angel, he would turn into a completely different person because he knew the Spirit of God would then manifest phenomenal healings.

People who have attended his meetings have said as the Holy Spirit moved on Brother Branham, he would operate in amazingly specific words of knowledge. Sometimes he would receive revelational gifts of the Spirit that were so precise he would spell out names of ailments and diseases.

I remember a number of years ago when Janet and I traveled to Cape Town, South Africa, to minister there. We stayed in the home of a couple who used to host Brother Branham as a guest. He would stay with this couple when he would conduct meetings on the military base in Cape Town.

"We had never seen anything like his meetings before," the couple told us of the Branham meetings. "When one of his crusades would end, workers would have to bring in full-sized trucks to haul away all the medical paraphernalia left behind. People would get healed in droves and leave behind braces, crutches, stretchers and wheelchairs. Everything you can think of was left behind because people didn't need it any more after they got healed."

Angel Delivers Healing to Cripple

God used an angel to deliver healing to a crippled man a few years back when we were in Germany doing a week of meetings with a minister friend.

An older gentleman, who looked to be about 70, hobbled and scooted up the center aisle and stopped in front of the platform in the middle of our friend's Bible message. The elderly man was permanently bowed over like the woman Jesus ministered to in Luke 13; all he could do was barely tilt his head to see where he was walking. He probably suffered from some form of crippling arthritis.

Even though it was the middle of the service, nobody told the crippled man to sit down. It was obvious that he had come for something important.

"Sir, what do you need?" the minister asked through an interpreter.

The crippled man immediately got down on his knees to worship the minister.

"Stand up!" the minister quickly said. "I'm not doing the healing around here. Jesus is the Healer. What do you need?"

Before the man could answer, suddenly his body began straightening upright. Janet and I were sitting on the front row, and we saw the whole thing. Not a single person touched him; not a single person prayed for him. Yet the elderly man straightened up quicker than you could imagine. Not only did he straighten up, but also he kept right on going up on his tiptoes. He looked like he was becoming airborne. *The guy is coming off the ground!* I remember thinking.

"Look at that! Look at that!" the minister said. "An angel has the man by the shoulders, and he's straightening the man up!"

The man looked startled and the expression on his face was like, *What's happening to me?* By then he was on his tiptoes, and it looked like something or someone was pulling him up by his shoulders. In seconds his body went from bent over where his only view was his feet to totally upright, normal and straight. Glory to God! The man went back to his seat perfectly healed.

> "LOOK AT THAT! LOOK AT THAT!" THE MINISTER SAID. "AN ANGEL HAS THE MAN BY THE SHOULDERS, AND HE'S STRAIGHTENING THE MAN UP!"

The angel wasn't doing the healing and neither was the minister, but God had a man preaching on healing and an angel bringing healing down from heaven. That's what I call a dynamic duo. God had healing delivered from heaven—right straight from the throne of God.

We found out later that the man was a WW II veteran in Hitler's army who was captured by the Soviets. He was taken as a prisoner to a Siberian war camp, where his job the entire time was to haul wood strapped to his back. For the duration of the camp, he was bent over day in and day out carrying wood. Obviously arthritis, years in the making, had settled in his back. But in a matter of seconds, an angel straightened the man's back and caused him to stand as straight and whole as anybody in the room.

I'm telling you what, angels will get involved in the healing ministry. We might as well get ready for it. There have been times I've ministered when I knew angels were working with me; sometimes you just know they're present. There will be times when angels show up and people will see them; most of the time people will not see them. Either way, God uses angels to assist with healing even though angels don't actually do the healing themselves. Angels are messengers sent by God to deliver healings that Jesus already purchased to repair the bodies of sick people.

Creative Miracles

There's no question that we'll see more and more healings in this hour, but we're also going to see an abundance of creative miracles. What's the difference between a healing and a miracle? A healing is when God fixes, repairs or mends a body part that isn't working right, whereas miracles are more creative in nature.

An example of a creative miracle would be God giving a new body part to someone—like a new arm or a leg—where there wasn't one before. We might as well get ready to hear testimonies of God moving in this miraculous realm because they're coming. Greater works than we've ever seen are coming—much, much greater works.

Angel Installs New Heart

I remember another meeting in Colorado where an angel delivered healing to an individual. The meeting had begun on Sunday with another minister, and we arrived Monday to hear the amazing testimony. In the middle of the service Sunday morning, the minister said, "Somebody here needs a *new* heart. Who is that? Come down to the front."

Our minister friend told us that a gentleman probably in his late 70s got up from his seat and walked toward the front, saying, "That's me! That's me!"

The elderly man told the crowd that he had traveled to the meeting from another state to visit the gravesite of his brother. "I was on my way to the cemetery to tell my brother, 'I'll be there soon!'" he said.

"My heart is so bad that I can't walk very far, hardly anywhere," the elderly man said. "Doctors have told me there's nothing they can do. They have said I would be a candidate for a heart transplant, but I wouldn't make it through surgery. So I just stay ready to go to heaven."

The minister said to him, "All I can tell you is that there has been an angel standing right over here by the piano since the beginning of the service with a new heart for somebody. He's not here to fix the old one; God sent him to put a new heart in you. You're the one!"

The elderly man raised his hands, and as the minister prayed for him, he fell to the floor under the power of God. Shortly thereafter, the man got up and returned to the relative's house where he was staying. He hadn't been able to carry his suitcase since he arrived in Colorado. The altitude there is higher and the air is thinner, and the man had a heart condition on top of that.

Usually he would pick up his suitcase and take one step before having to put the suitcase down to catch his breath. Then he would pick up the suitcase, put it up on the next step and stand there waiting to catch his breath again. The older gentleman continued this way until he reached the top step. But on that Sunday when he returned form the meeting where he had received a new heart, things were dramatically different. The elderly man got back to the house and *ran* up and down the stairs.

> THE MINISTER SAID TO HIM, "ALL I CAN TELL YOU IS THAT THERE HAS BEEN AN ANGEL STANDING RIGHT OVER HERE BY THE PIANO SINCE THE BEGINNING OF THE SERVICE WITH A NEW HEART FOR SOMEBODY.

Excitedly he returned to the church service that night and shared with the people, "I just wanted to let you know that I went by the cemetery to my brother's grave again. I know he's not really there anyway, but I still wanted to go by and tell him that it would be a long time now before I would get to heaven to see him. I told him that I've got a lot more years to live now because Jesus gave me a brand new heart!"

Jesus is the Healer, and Jesus is the One who bought and paid for our healing, but thank God for angels involved in the healing ministry. I believe there are many more of these testimonies to come as we approach harvest.

Angel Realigns Bones

We were in another meeting in California with this same minister in the mid 1980s where we saw angels assist again in delivering healing. The minister had a word of knowledge and called out this description. "There's somebody here who was in an automobile accident that messed up your whole body. It's left your skeletal system in bad shape. Whoever you are, come up here!"

> "THERE'S AN ANGEL HOLDING HER BY HER FEET AND STRAIGHTENING OUT HER ENTIRE SKELETAL SYSTEM RIGHT NOW."

A woman began walking down the aisle, and as she approached the front, you could tell she was moving really slow as if she were wracked with pain. But before the minister could speak to her or pray for her, she got three or four steps away from the front and fell to the floor. The woman lay on the floor under the power of God.

Then the only way I can describe what happened is that all of the sudden something took hold of her uneven legs and began pushing them back and forth, back and forth. I watched the whole thing, and it was a movement that a person couldn't do by herself. I mean the woman's whole body was rocking.

"Look at that," the minister said, "There's an angel holding her by her feet and straightening out her entire skeletal system right now." Within minutes, the woman was on her feet, and her legs were the same length. She was perfectly well, perfectly healed instantly—and no longer in pain.

The truth is, these things should not only happen in one man's ministry. We ought to expect these sorts of miracles in the Church world all the time. *We don't have to see angels working in order for them to be working, but we should expect them to be working all the time.* Whenever we have healing and miracle services, we should expect angels to be involved because we see precedent for it in God's Word.

Angels Straightens Spine

A few years back I remember conducting a healing service with friends of ours who lived as missionaries in Poland. Before the service began, the Spirit of God said to me, "There will be angels working in here tonight." *OK, fine with me,* I thought. *I'll take all the help I can get.*

We prayed for many, many people that night who wanted healing in their bodies and came forward for prayer. One man in particular came up after the service with an amazing testimony. He said that even though there was an interpreter, he didn't understand the invitation to come to the front for prayer to receive salvation or healing. He explained that he had never been before in a service where anyone gave out a word of knowledge or prayed for the sick.

The man went on to explain that he had been diagnosed with tumors up and down his spine. "Even though I did not come up for prayer," he said, "I felt a large hand that I could not see on my back. All the tumors are gone! I've checked! They're all gone!" Praise God! Angels ministered to people that night in and out of the healing line.

I expect it all the time. I won't be a bit surprised if in the days to come folks sit in church and see angels walking the aisles delivering healings. Why not? That should not be the exception to the rule; it ought to be the rule. Whether people see angels or not, we ought to welcome them in our services. We're coming into a healing wave so big and so strong that people won't just get healed by getting into a healing line, but people will get healed the minute they step onto the church property. Let's expect it!

New Hearts

Several years ago we knew a lady who began to develop heart problems. Her doctor had diagnosed a pretty major blockage in her heart, and it was a serious thing. She and her husband began to pray about it and believe God for healing.

> "I WAS PRAYING AND SUDDENLY IT FELT LIKE A HAND WENT DOWN ON THE INSIDE OF ME, MOVED SOMETHING AND TOOK OUT THAT HEART BLOCKAGE."

"Then one day," she said, "I was praying and suddenly it felt like a hand went down on the inside of me, moved something and took out that heart blockage." For a fact, the blockage instantly disappeared, and the woman lived many, many, many more years before she stepped over into heaven with absolutely no blockage in her heart or heart problem. She simply got up in years and stepped over to heaven.

What do you suppose she felt that was "like a hand" and fixed her heart? *Was it Jesus or an angel?* somebody might ask. Who cares? Either way, it's good; either way, she got healed.

I know of two more cases where an angel has brought a brand new heart into a church service. I don't mean an angel fixed an old one that didn't work well; I mean an angel put in a brand new one. Medical science couldn't figure out what happened. Yet, God designed our bodies, and He's well able to repair parts or replace them with new ones.

Chapter Six

Divine Connections, Guidance, Encouragement and More

The more we expect angels to work in our lives, the more we'll experience amazing, spectacular help from heaven. From the beginning, angels have been involved in delivering the supernatural into the lives of believers. God uses angels to arrange supernatural set ups and divine connections and deliver guidance and encouragement. We need to expect this help kind of help daily because our expectation is God's invitation to make it happen.

In Acts 8 we read how an angel was on assignment bringing guidance to Philip and arranging divine connections and appointments for him. The evangelist had gone to Samaria to conduct a city wide crusade, preaching the death, burial and resurrection of Jesus to the people. There were signs, wonders and miracles that got everybody's attention. The city was shaken by the power of God, and there was great joy in the city.

Then notice what happened afterward.

Acts 8:26-29 (NKJV)
26 Now an angel of the Lord spoke to Philip, saying, "Arise and go toward the south along the road which goes down from Jerusalem to Gaza." This is desert.

> 27 So he arose and went. And behold, a man of Ethiopia, a eunuch of great authority under Candace the queen of the Ethiopians, who had charge of all her treasury, and had come to Jerusalem to worship,
>
> 28 was returning. And sitting in his chariot, he was reading Isaiah the prophet.
>
> 29 Then the Spirit said to Philip, "Go near and overtake this chariot."

After the city-wide crusade, an angel told Philip to, "Get up and get going!" But did you notice that even though the angel came to give him guidance, the scripture did not say the angel *appeared* to Philip? It said the angel *spoke* to him. We really don't know whether the angel appeared to him and spoke to him or whether the angel only spoke to him.

Either way, the angel got pretty specific with Philip and said, "Arise and go toward the south along the road which goes down from Jerusalem to Gaza." I find it interesting that the angel didn't just say, "Hey, I'm here with glad tidings!" No, the angel was sent with detailed instructions and sent to arrange a divine connection.

When Philip caught up with the Ethiopian eunuch, he was reading the book of Isaiah but not understanding a word of it. The Holy Spirit spoke to Phillip and told him to go join the man in the chariot. So Phillip jumped in the chariot and said to the eunuch, "Do you understand what you're reading?"

"How can I possibly understand this book unless some man explains it to me," the eunuch answered.

You know the story. Phillip began to explain the scriptures to the eunuch and preach Jesus Christ to him. It was no time at all before the Ethiopian eunuch got born again and baptized with water. Legend tells us that when the eunuch returned home, he took revival back to the whole of North Africa. Thank God there are times when we think we've reached one person, but we've actually reached an entire community of people. We may not always know the full extent of what we've accomplished for the kingdom, but God knows.

Notice here that the angel assigned to help Philip was involved in different facets of helping him. The angel was involved in helping Philip preach Jesus Christ. The angel was involved in giving directions and guidance. The angel was involved in setting up divine connections and appointments and all of the above are scriptural. And just as God used an angel to help Philip in different ways, God can and will use angels to move in any or all of these ways in your life as well.

A Divine Connection Leads to Salvation

The interesting thing is, most of the time we don't even recognize divine connections and supernatural set ups are in motion while they're happening to us. Sometimes we don't know until a long time afterward that God set us up or supernaturally arranged divine appointments and circumstances or connected us with people to benefit us or them or both. I can think of times in my own life when it was a month later, a year later, or even five years down the road before I recognized what God had actually done for me.

Amos 3:3 explains a lot when it says, "Can two walk together, except they be agreed?" The Amplified Translation says of the scripture, "Do two walk together except they make an appointment…?" I'm a firm believer in divine appointments; they have changed my life.

Divine appointments can be especially important in getting people born again. In fact, I can say from experience that when you believe for the salvation of your relatives and friends, don't just pray, "God save them!" Jesus already did that 2,000 years ago on the cross. What folks need to hear is the good news of salvation and how to receive what Jesus already provided for them. They need God to arrange a divine connection with a laborer who will present the message of salvation in a way they will receive.

That's what happened to me. My mom prayed and prayed for me. She got filled with the Holy Spirit praying for me. In fact, she went to all kinds of women's meetings and would ask other women friends to pray for me, too. As a college student I remember thinking, *I wish she'd get those ladies off my back.* Life was miserable for me from the moment my mom got all the women in her Aglow prayer meetings to pray for me until the day I got born again. Then again, when you're not right with God, it's probably a good thing to be miserable.

Eventually my mom gave up trying to figure out how to get me right with God, and she finally turned the whole thing over to God. "Lord, You find somebody to talk to Him," she prayed. And He did.

He always does when we put our confidence in Him, and He knows who an individual will listen to a whole lot better than we do. I was a college student minding my own business and trying my best to stay away from what God had for my life. Like many people, I was afraid of what He might ask me to do.

Yet one night I landed in one of God's divine connections. I belonged to a judo club at college, and I walked into the gym looking for some practice. I saw this guy who had the same rank belt I had but was about half my size, so I decided he was a good candidate. That was a big mistake.

I walked over to him and bowed. He bowed in return, and we stepped out on the mat. Thirty minutes later, I limped off the mat beaten, bloodied and bruised. The guy beat the thunder out of me, and I just wanted to get out of there.

A couple of weeks later, I was walking through my dorm and saw this same guy from the judo club coming down the hall. He recognized me, so I walked over to say hello. I thought it was better to be friends; I knew for sure I didn't want him as an enemy the way he beat on me.

"What are you doing in this dorm," I asked.

"They just transferred me to your dorm," he said. "I got moved clear across campus."

We visited for a few minutes and then he asked, "Since I'm kind of new in the dorm here, do you know anything going on around here this weekend?"

"I don't know. Why?" I asked.

"If you don't know about it already," he said, "There's a really good place you ought to go."

"Where's that?" I asked.

"There's a meeting going down at the civic center with a man named Leighton Ford. He's an associate of Billy Graham, and I think you ought to go listen to him."

I remember thinking, *Oh, no, you're one of those.*

After that the guy just wouldn't leave me alone, and I couldn't forget about what he said because he earned my respect big time on the judo mat. I just couldn't argue with him. About three days later I finally said, "Listen, if you'll leave me alone, I'll go to your meeting. OK?"

"OK," he said. "If you go, I'll leave you alone, but I'm not leaving you alone until you go."

Long story short, I went to that meeting, and I'm very glad I did. I walked down the aisle and got saved that night. That guy, that meeting, that divine connection changed the entire course of my life.

So trust God for your loved ones. Usually He picks out somebody you wouldn't pick out or know to pick out to talk to them. Bind the devil off of your loved ones, and trust God for the people you're praying about. God

> GOD HAS ANGELS DOWN HERE WHO CAN GET BUSY ARRANGING AND REARRANGING AND CONNECTING AND MOVING AROUND ALL KINDS OF SCHEDULES, JOBS AND THINGS TO SUPERNATURALLY BRING THE RIGHT LABORERS TO YOUR LOVED ONES.

has angels down here who can get busy arranging and rearranging and connecting and moving around all kinds of schedules, jobs and things to supernaturally bring the right laborers to your loved ones.

We need to understand that angels know what's going on down here. If evil spirits and familiar spirits know various details about people's lives, why wouldn't God's angels? Think about it. If evil spirits can know about people's lives and feed information to the psychic network without the wisdom of God and without the Holy Spirit, then how much more can angels know what's going on and set things up for us?

I'm telling you what, God wants to work in our lives, and I believe He wants to work in ways we've never before seen. But He needs our expectation, and that's one reason it's important to talk about the ways God desires to move. I believe He's got divine appointments for every Christian, and He has angels busy setting them up.

God moving the guy into my dorm was the first divine connection I recognized in my life. I knew right then that the Holy Spirit was on my case. But from that day in November 1972 to today, I've seen God establish countless divine connections and setups in my life and the lives of many others.

Sometimes you just know what He's doing, and sometimes you don't. Sometimes you recognize the importance of meeting a certain person, and sometimes you simply run across the path of a person and don't think a thing about it. Then years later, you see what a supernatural moment it really was.

There are times I've just had a leading or a witness to do business with a certain person, or I've had an unction to follow a particular pathway to do business with someone. Then later on, I have an opportunity to get the person born again or get the person healed. I'm telling you that God is in the business of divine appointments. Sometimes they're for you and me, and sometimes they're set up for the other person. God knows, and that's why He has angels busy making appointments.

A Divine Appointment for Cornelius

Look with me at Acts 10 to see how angels were involved in another Christian's life.

Acts 10:1-6

1 There was a certain man in Caesarea called Cornelius, a centurion of what was called the Italian Regiment,

2 A devout man and one who feared God with all his household, who gave alms generously to the people, and prayed to God always.

3 About the ninth hour of the day he saw clearly in a vision an angel of God coming in and saying to him, "Cornelius!" 4 And when he observed him, he was afraid, and said, "What is it, lord?" So he said to him, "Your prayers and your alms have come up for a memorial before God.

5 Now send men to Joppa, and send for Simon whose surname is Peter.

6 He is lodging with Simon, a tanner, whose house is by the sea. He will tell you what you must do."

An angel brought Cornelius a message with instructions from heaven and arranged several divine appointments all at the same time. "You've done good!" the angel told Cornelius. "You're a man of prayer, you're a giver, and it pleases God." Then the angel said, "While you're at it, send men to Joppa. Go find a guy there named Peter. Track him down by the sea side."

We cannot expect angels to preach the gospel—that's not their job. That's our job. But angels sure will put a person in contact with somebody who can preach the gospel. Angels are out and about influencing us and influencing other people for good. I believe they often move us into places where we can make divine connections capable of changing the very course of our lives.

> ANGELS ARE OUT AND ABOUT INFLUENCING US AND INFLUENCING OTHER PEOPLE FOR GOOD. I BELIEVE THEY OFTEN MOVE US INTO PLACES WHERE WE CAN MAKE DIVINE CONNECTIONS CAPABLE OF CHANGING THE VERY COURSE OF OUR LIVES.

Have you ever just happened to land at the right place at the right time and open the right door to meet the right person? If you haven't, trust God that you will because He'll put angels to work on it right now.

God arranged divine connections in Acts 10. Of course this passage of scripture was concerning salvation, which is the most important connection, without a doubt. Then again, if God can make divine appointments and connections to lead people to salvation, why can't He make divine appointments and connections for those people who are already saved? Why should it stop with salvation? Why shouldn't it increase with salvation?

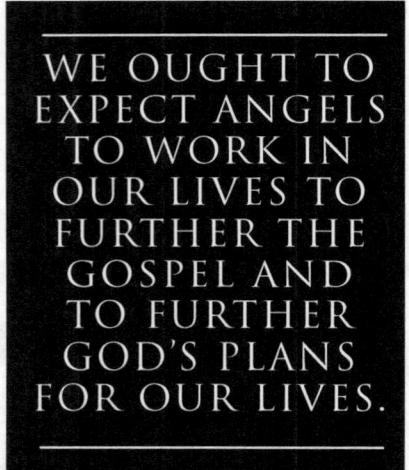

WE OUGHT TO EXPECT ANGELS TO WORK IN OUR LIVES TO FURTHER THE GOSPEL AND TO FURTHER GOD'S PLANS FOR OUR LIVES.

In Acts 10 the angel goes on to tell Cornelius to find Simon Peter who would give him further instructions. Later on, when Cornelius gave his testimony, he quoted the angel as saying Simon will "…tell you words by which you and all your household will be saved" (Acts 11:14 NKJV). Cornelius did as he was told and sent men to find Peter.

Meanwhile, Peter was on the rooftop praying around lunchtime. About that time he fell into a trance and heard the Holy Spirit speak to him.

> **Acts 10:29-20**
> 19 While Peter thought on the vision, the Spirit said unto him, Behold, three men seek thee.
> 20 Arise therefore, and get thee down, and go with them, doubting nothing: for I have sent them.

It looks to me like God was working on both ends. When Peter went with the men, he found a house full of Gentiles, and before you know it, the gospel was poured out on the Gentile world at Cornelius' house. It spread all over the world from there. Isn't it interesting that the gospel spreading to the Gentiles was the direct result of an angel bringing guidance and arranging a divine appointment? We ought to expect angels to work in our lives to further the gospel and to further God's plans for our lives.

No matter your profession or career, you ought to expect angels to be at work in your life. If you're in any kind of business, you ought to have angels connecting you with customers, clients and patients. You ought to have angels working in your life no matter what the field or ministry is where God has called you. If angels can make divine appointments for Cornelius and Simon Peter, they can make them for you. If angels can make divine appointments for Phillip and an Ethiopian eunuch, then they can make divine appointments for you and the business or job or ministry that God has laid out for you.

Angels know things by the mind of God or they know things simply because they're down here on earth. Either way, angels are in the know. "Well then," somebody asks, "should I believe for God to help me or should I believe for angels to help me?" GOD.

We must always believe and trust God for answers or divine appointments and connections, guidance and for everything we need from God's Word; that's what God's Word instructs us to do. If God wants to use an angel to deliver what we need, that's fine. If He doesn't, that's fine, too, because that would mean God has another way, a better way. God always chooses the best way to do whatever He does.

Angelic Guidance

In the area of guidance, the vast majority of the time God leads and guides Christians by the inward witness of the Spirit of God. But God is God, and He can add, enhance and make exceptions anytime He wants within the boundaries of His Word.

For instance, in Acts 8 an angel told Philip, "Go down to Gaza." But then the Spirit of God told Philip what he was to do once he got there. You might wonder, *Why did the angel give him a direction? Why didn't the Spirit of God tell him the whole instruction? Or why didn't Philip have an inward witness?* I don't know. Yet, you will see this same thing happening from time to time throughout scriptures.

In Acts 10 we just read that an angel showed up and told Cornelius to send men to Joppa to find a man named Peter. Why did an angel bring that message? I don't know, but he did. Over on the other side, why was Peter instructed in a vision? I don't know, but he was.

What about the angel that warned Paul of a major storm in Acts 27? Paul was on board a ship that had been sailing in a storm for about two weeks. Before they left, Paul warned them, "Sirs, I perceive this voyage to be with much hurt and danger." Unfortunately, the sailors didn't listen to him; Paul was only a prisoner in their minds and they weren't open to his advice.

But after two weeks in a serious and violent storm, Paul finally rebuked them, saying, "You should have listened to me before we left, but you refused to do it. Now look at the mess you've gotten us into." Apparently Paul was one of those I-told-you-so guys. But after letting the sailors have it, this is what Paul said.

Acts 27:22-25

22 And now I exhort you to be of good cheer: for there shall be no loss of any man's life among you, but of the ship.

23 For there stood by me this night the angel of God, whose I am, and whom I serve,

24 Saying, Fear not, Paul; thou must be brought before Caesar: and, lo, God hath given thee all them that sail with thee.

25 Wherefore, sirs, be of good cheer: for I believe God, that it shall be even as it was told me.

Notice that Paul did not say *Jesus appeared to me* or even *the Holy Spirit said to me*. He said *an angel told me*. Actually, he said "…there stood by me an angel…" so he either perceived or saw that angel next to him. Why did an angel bring that specific direction? I don't know, but he did.

Let's look at it this way. We saw this same precedent in Acts 8, we saw it in Acts 10, and we saw it in Acts 27. That's three witnesses. The Bible says in the mouth of two or three witnesses let every word be established. With this kind of proof in the New Testament, we can expect angelic activity to operate today in all these same facets for us.

I remember an instance of an angel guiding me and helping me when I was in college that I've never forgotten. It's really stayed with me, and I can remember it almost like it was yesterday. Actually, I can still close my eyes and just see the exact location.

It was one of those times when I was at a crossroad in my life, and I heard a voice that was so loud it was almost audible. I was alone in my car at the time, but the voice was so loud I looked around to see who was in the car with me.

If I had made the wrong decision on that occasion, it would have been disastrous. I don't need to go into all the details, but the point is that I always thought that God had spoken to me. Yet, as I look back now that I'm a few years down the road, I realize that it was an angel. Thank God for that angel who literally saved my life.

I don't mean the angel helped me a little; I mean the angel absolutely saved my life. I wasn't even born again at the time; I wasn't walking with God. I wasn't even close to it, but thank God for angels.

There have been other times when I sensed angelic help in my life or when I've sensed a being standing right next to me. If you look to see who's there, you get in the flesh and miss it. Yet, there have been numerous occasions when there was a presence near me, and all of a sudden, I would hear words of specific direction in my spirit. Every time that has happened, the direction has been exactly right on. Of course, if it's an angel, the direction will never oppose the Word of God.

Does the supernatural guidance that angels brought to Philip, Cornelius and Paul mean that *every time* we need direction in life we should wait for an angel to bring it from heaven? No. When we make decisions, should we wait to see if God wants an angel to bring us direction?

No. Romans 8:14 clearly says that the sons—and daughters—of God are led by the Spirit of God because God is a spirit, and He bears witness with our spirits.

If you're a son or daughter of God, then you should be led by the Spirit of God in all the affairs of your life. If God wants to do something different in a specific situation or use an angel to bring guidance, He'll let you know. Meanwhile, you do everything the Bible says you should do, and God will add on top as He decides is needed or not needed.

Angels Help Unload a Lemon

God also knows that sometimes the help we need from angels isn't spiritual help at all. In fact, *angelic help is always supernatural, but it is not always spiritual.*

I remember how angels helped me supernaturally unload a lemon of a vehicle a number of years ago. Before leaving my home state of Michigan to enroll in Bible school in 1974 in Tulsa, Oklahoma, I had sold my vehicle. I knew I would need to buy another one in Tulsa. Long story short, I ended up hearing about a great car deal down in Dallas. From the moment I heard about it, I wanted it. I drooled over the telephone when I heard it was a 1968 XKE Jaguar. I told the guy in Dallas that I would drive down the next weekend to pick it up.

> **ANGELIC HELP IS ALWAYS SUPERNATURAL, BUT IT IS NOT ALWAYS SPIRITUAL.**

Looking back I really missed God's leading when I bought that car. I clearly recognize now I had a check in my spirit or a leading not to purchase it, but back then I didn't know I was supposed to be led by the Spirit of God let alone what a check in my spirit was. I didn't know that God will keep us out of trouble if we let Him.

So I bought the very yellow car, and time would tell that the color was fitting because it was a major lemon. On one hand, it was a beautiful car, but on the other hand, anything that could go wrong with it did go wrong with it.

Three or four things even broke on the way home from Dallas to Tulsa. Then in the three months I had it, the clutch went out twice, the brakes went out twice and the battery went dead. It wasn't long before I was known as the guy with the Jag that never ran.

I will say that car helped me learn the bus routes all over Tulsa because my car never ran. I was a pretty decent mechanic, but I didn't have a lot of time for that while I was in school studying. That's not to mention that the car was British so it was built differently than cars I was used to working on and finding parts wasn't easy.

Finally, I decided I would take the car back to Michigan during my Christmas break from school. So there I was in a little two-seat convertible in December driving to Michigan in a car not designed for snow. Somewhere on the other side of St. Louis, I landed in one of those Midwestern blizzards, and all of the sudden, I realized the car and I were in big trouble.

Even in first gear the thing would not run under 40 mph, so there I was driving 40 mph in 25-mph traffic. I was in the passing lane pioneering new territory and blazing a new trail with snow flying everywhere. Other drivers were aggravated because I was blowing past everybody on the road.

I tried to motion to them and convey my problem, but that definitely didn't work. Worse yet, I knew if I slowed down, the car would die, and then I would be stuck frozen in a ditch for the next three days. So I continued my trek at 40 mph in the passing lane with a car that sat barely off the ground.

Keep in mind that I wasn't driving over the snow; I was plowing *through* it. It was a ride I'll never forget, not to mention that by the time I finally drove into my hometown, the clutch had quit working. You know, it's tricky to shift without using a clutch. I could not stop for red lights or stop signs or I would be stuck.

Finally, as I pulled into the outskirts of my hometown, I pulled up in front of a real estate company my dad owned and landed in a snow bank. I slapped a for sale sign on the front window and left, hoping never to see it again.

Now when you think about it, a two-seat convertible is not a real salable item in Michigan in the middle of December. By that time next to nothing worked on the vehicle, and basically if a person bought the car, he or she would need to buy a mechanic to go along with it.

My brother-in-law owned an extra vehicle at the time that was not running really well, and he told me if I could get it running I could take it back to Tulsa. So I enjoyed Christmas and left the Jag sitting in the snow. I told my dad before I left town, "If anyone wants it, sell it to them." You couldn't even see the for sale sign on its windshield because the vehicle was still buried in deep snow.

Driving back to Oklahoma, I remember praying about the car. I said, "Lord, You and I both know I missed it buying that Jag. I know I did. You tried to tell me, but I just didn't know enough to listen, and I've paid the price for it now. Forgive me. I just didn't know any better; it wasn't intentional. I didn't know You were trying to lead me differently."

Then I began to pray, "You know, Lord, somebody wants that car. I don't know why, and I don't know who, but I believe somebody wants that car. I believe it's somebody who has money to fix it and maintain it. So, Lord, we need to find a person with money who wants that car. I call it sold in Jesus' name.

"Now, Lord, Your Word says ministering spirits are sent forth to minister *to* and *for* those who are heirs of salvation. Ministering spirits know everything going on around here by the mind of Christ and the wisdom of God, so maybe You will use angels to locate someone who wants the Jag. Lord, I believe there has got to be one human in the nation out there somewhere who wants my car."

About a week later, somebody pulled up at my father's real estate office and said he wanted to buy the car for his wife. Being the ethical businessman he is, my dad laughingly said, "Oh, no you don't."

"Really, I do want the car," the guy said.

"Well, you'll need a mechanic to get it to run," my dad explained right upfront.

"Listen, that's not a problem," the guy said. "I understand these cars, and I know how they're made. I also know my wife has always dreamed of a car just like this, and I want to get it for her. I've got plenty of money to fix it. I'm just glad to find one." So he wrote out a deposit check and said he would send a tow truck to pick it up.

The guy didn't negotiate or flinch on the price at all, and I had added $500 over what I had paid for it just for my misery. Would you believe a few days later the phone kept ringing in my dad's office over that car? People started bidding on it, and in three days, three people called wanting the car.

One guy called from another state and said, "I understand you've got an XKE Jaguar for sale. I'll take it sight unseen. I want it."

"Sorry," my dad said. "I've already got a deposit check holding it."

"Whatever they offered you, I'll give you more," the guy said.

"No, I cannot do that. I don't do business that way," Dad said. "If the other guy backs out, I'll get back with you. But right now, as far as I know, it's sold."

No wonder the guy wanted it. Today the car would be worth a lot of money; I saw one priced awhile back at more than $30,000, and I only paid around $2,200 for it. If only I had known and had the money, the time and the patience, it could have been a valuable investment.

Then again, I learned a much more valuable lesson about listening to the Holy Spirit for guidance. I learned how God can dispatch angels to help us, and I learned we've got a Holy Spirit network down here with angels making divine connections for us.

Angels Ready to Help You

Angels know what's going on down here; they know everybody in the world. They know who's looking for what and who's talking about what. They know how to give directions. They know how to find people, and they know how to make divine appointments.

I asked God to send angels to help me, and He did. Within a few weeks, I had people bidding on a lemon of a convertible buried in the snow. Why? Because we have ministering spirits—angels—sent to minister for those who are heirs of salvation.

I've heard people say, "I'm not sure God can help me in this situation. I got myself into this mess, and I'll have to get myself out." But we get ourselves into all kinds of situations, and it's Jesus Christ who still rescues us every time. God doesn't mind that; He wants to bail you out of all kinds of things. Bottom line, God wants to prosper His children, and He wants angels involved in what we're doing.

> THANK GOD FOR ANGELS ARRANGING SCHEDULES AND SETTING UP DIVINE APPOINTMENTS THAT WILL HELP YOU RUN YOUR RACE, FINISH YOUR COURSE AND MAKE YOU A BLESSING TO OTHERS.

Have you got something you need to sell or something you need God to arrange? Trust God, and if He needs to loose angels to work in your life, your situations and your circumstances, He can and will do it. Begin to thank God and expect Him to arrange the course of your life with divine appointments, connections and set ups. It will change the course of your whole life. Begin to call in divine appointments for your life or your business or your ministry. Call in divine connections from the North, the South, the East and the West.

Thank the Lord for angels finding folks who need what you've got and who have what you need. Thank God for divine connections and appointments concerning jobs. Thank God that you supernaturally meet people wherever you go and whatever you do. Thank God that you meet the right people at the right time and are led in all the affairs of life. Thank God for angels arranging schedules and setting up divine appointments that will help you run your race, finish your course and make you a blessing to others.

Realize that if you've committed your life to Jesus Christ, there are good things waiting for you around every corner. Good things are waiting for you every morning when you wake up. Good things are waiting for you everyday when you break for lunch. Good things are waiting for you everyday when you head home from work. Good things—divine directions, divine set ups, divine appointments and divine connections—are waiting for you.

Angels can help us in so many different ways—all the ways the devil tries to attack Christians. We're all aware that the devil attacks our bodies, our finances and our minds. He tries so hard to get us to slow down and quit. Basically, if he cannot get in one way, he'll try another. But God knows how to stop him in his tracks, and God has a heavenly host of angels helping Him help us.

Angel Sent to 'Garrison the Mind'

I remember years ago a real attack came against my mind, and God used an angel to turn things around. I was letting myself get stressed, and it was my own fault. I had never had any trouble like that before or after, but at that particular time a real attack had come against my mind. I've always been of sound mind, but at that time it was almost to the point where I couldn't think a straight thought. My mind seemed clouded.

There were times I would sit down and try to focus on my Bible, reading a line at a time to try to keep my mind going right. It was a demonic attack. I told Janet that the only way I could describe it was like there were bats flying around outside my head.

Right around that same time, a friend of ours called and said, "I've been praying for you guys, and the weird thing is every time I get to praying I keep praying out the word *bats*."

"Keep praying," I said.

Somebody says, "You're a minister, and you've had attacks?" Hello! Another person told me one time, "Man, I'm going through some really rough times, but you wouldn't understand. You're a preacher." I wish that were true, but here's the real truth. Everybody gets to stand in faith alike; there are no exceptions. The devil is no respecter of persons. The devil attacks ministers, too. The good news is that God can deliver all of us out of whatever attacks the devil throws our way.

> ONE DAY WHEN I WAS PRAYING DURING THIS SAME TIME FRAME, I SUDDENLY SENSED THAT A SUPERNATURAL BEING HAD ENTERED THE ROOM.

One day when I was praying during this same time frame, I suddenly sensed that a supernatural being had entered the room. There was just this wonderful presence that came in the room. Out of the corner of my eye, I got a flash of somebody standing there, but as I turned to look, I missed it. I didn't sense that it was Jesus, but I knew it was not the devil. You can tell the difference.

I got quiet and all of a sudden I heard these words down inside, "I'm an angel sent from the throne of God to garrison your mind." I'm telling you what, it was just like *snap!* My mind instantly cleared.

I remember thinking, *I don't know what garrison means, but this is good.* I went right away and looked up the word *garrison*, which means *to stand guard over, to watch over.*

The angel went on to say, "I was commissioned by so and so," and named a particular person I knew to be a person of prayer. I still had to exercise my faith and fight the good fight of faith against thoughts, but I noticed an immediate difference. Months later I saw this individual whose name the angel had mentioned and so I asked a few questions.

"Let me ask you something," I said. "Back a few months, were you praying for us?"

"Yes, I was," she said.

"Were you praying anything specific?" I asked.

"No. I would simply get to praying in tongues, and you would kind of come up in my heart, so I would pray for you and Janet. There was nothing really specific, though."

I kept waiting to hear the person say, "Yeah, I got over in the spirit, and I commissioned an angel to go to you." But there was nothing like that; the person simply prayed in tongues.

That was a major revelation to me. Think about it. When we get to praying for folks, we don't necessarily have to send angels to do anything. If we'll just pray with unction, God will take care of it all. We may have no idea what we're praying or what's being accomplished when we're praying, and that's fine. If we just pray in the Holy Spirit, God will take care of the situation the way He wants to take care of it.

> I GOT QUIET AND ALL OF A SUDDEN I HEARD THESE WORDS DOWN INSIDE, "I'M AN ANGEL SENT FROM THE THRONE OF GOD TO GARRISON YOUR MIND."

I thought, *Isn't it interesting that the person didn't even really set out to pray for me, but her prayers touched the throne of God just the same.* And God sent forth an angel. That ought to be a real boost to your prayer life; it was to mine.

This person didn't know what she was praying about, and she didn't go to the throne of God requesting, "God, send an angel! A friend of mine needs a miracle down here!" No, she just prayed in other tongues, and heaven responded. I'm thankful God dispatched a big angel to come down and garrison my mind. The angel was good at his job, and he's been doing it ever since.

Now keep in mind that while God sent supernatural help, I still had to do my part and fight the good fight of faith. I still had to take my stance and still had to believe God "casting down imaginations, and every high thing that exalteth itself against the knowledge of God, and bringing into captivity every thought to the obedience of Christ" (2 Corinthians 10:5).

That's right! The Bible tells you to pull down strongholds, which does not mean you find the highest hill outside your city and scream at devils. It doesn't mean you get in an airplane so you can go to another level of the atmosphere and pull down devils over cities. No, the only strongholds you'll ever have to deal with are the ones locked between your ears. I'm talking about thoughts and imaginations that try to lodge in your thinking.

The thing is, sometimes when people are attacked mentally or emotionally, they don't receive the help they need from God because they think God is mad at them. But God has always been in the business of helping people and encouraging people—even ministers.

Supernatural Encouragement

In 1 Kings 19, God sent an angel to minister encouragement to the prophet Elijah, who had become frustrated and discouraged. Actually, the prophet Elijah had been on a roll. He called down rain. He called down a drought. He called down fire. He unplugged the psychic network. He killed the false prophets and the prophets of Baal. He was supernaturally fed by ravens, supernaturally fed by a widow woman and supernaturally raised her son from the dead.

The man had a really good three-year run, but unfortunately, then he ran out of vision. Suddenly, he didn't know what else to do, and he became discouraged. Jezebel wanted to kill him, so he ran for his life. Finally, he ended up alone out in a field where he fell down and prayed to die.

While Elijah had fallen asleep under the tree, God sent an angel to encourage him. Verses 5-6 say the angel gave him water and cake. It must have been supernatural angel food cake, because the Bible said he lived off the strength of it for 40 days and 40 nights.

Then what? Did God scold him? No, God didn't do anything of the sort. Some people seem to think if they get discouraged that God will swat them and say, "Quit having a pity party. Get up and act like a man." But instead, God sent an angel to encourage Elijah.

Do you realize what this means? It means when you are hit with hard times, God will help you, too. He will send angels to help you. When things get a little difficult, situations get a little tight or folks are after you, remember that God is on your side. I'm so glad in times of distress that God doesn't get aggravated with us.

Sometimes sickness or poverty or another problem tries to attack you or your family, and you are a little discouraged in your soul. Sometimes your mind, will and emotions get discouraged. Yet, God does not say, "What's the matter with you? I thought you were a faith person." No, not at all.

Look at how God handled Elijah. One minute this major prophet of the land had called down fire and rain, but the next minute he was lying in the field praying to die. God never says, "OK, I'm through with you, boy." No, that's not our God. He sent an angel to take care of Elijah and to encourage him.

> **THERE ARE TEN THOUSAND TIMES TEN THOUSAND AND THOUSANDS AND THOUSANDS MORE ANGELS THAT GOD CAN CALL UPON TO BRING YOU ENCOURAGEMENT WHEN YOU NEED IT.**

I'm glad to know that there are ten thousand times ten thousand and thousands and thousands more angels that God can call upon to bring you encouragement when you need it. If you're encountering stressful situations or experiencing stressful times, then know that God has help for you. Expect God to send angels to bring comfort to you.

Angel Ministers to Grieving Mother

There are certain facets of angelic help most people have totally failed to recognize. I remember hearing how an angel helped a couple overtaken with grief, and it really opened my eyes to the many avenues where God uses angels to help us.

During World War II, the parents of a young soldier received news that their son had been tragically killed. The parents were devastated to lose their son and a spirit of grief came on the boy's mother particularly.

The mother was born again, filled with the Spirit and the love of God was in her, yet at the same time, she was absolutely overcome with grief. We all grieve when we lose someone we love, and that's to be expected; there's nothing wrong with grieving. Yet the Bible instructs Christians not to grieve as the world does (1 Thessalonians 4:13). People in the world get consumed with grief, and it ruins their lives. But when the loved one of a Christian passes to the other side, we have confidence that we will see the person again. We know that we're only separated for a time, but we will be reunited in heaven.

As this woman sat agonizing over the death of her son one afternoon in her home, a young man knocked on the front door. The mother answered the door and felt led to invite in the visitor. Take into account that this situation occurred in a small town in the 1940s, and things were different back then. In those days people were a lot more comfortable inviting strangers into their homes.

Without speaking a single word, the young man entered and walked through the house turning face down every picture of the son along the way. Amazingly enough, this young man knew where every picture was located in the whole house; the young man didn't miss a single one. Then he turned and walked out of the house. When he did, the spirit of grief completely broke off the mother, and she was a different person from that day forward.

How could a stranger know where every picture of the son was located in the couple's home? I don't think anybody could—*except an angel*. The truth is, there are an awful lot of things that we have not tapped in to concerning angelic activity, but I believe we're coming into an hour and a day when we're ready for angelic help like we've never experienced before.

Chapter Seven

ANGELS BRING IN THE MONEY

There's no question that as long as you live on this earth, you will have plenty of opportunities to trust God for provision and to meet your financial needs. And there's no question that God is ready to meet your financial needs, but have you ever wondered where God gets the money? After all, God hasn't set up a printing press in heaven, and He doesn't rain money down on us.

I can tell you that He won't grow a money tree in your backyard that sprouts 100 dollar bills on every branch. If He does, you let me know about it, so I can plant one of those trees in my backyard. No, God doesn't work that way because He's not a counterfeiter.

God won't get in your computer and mess with the numbers so He can transfer money into your bank account either. Even though the Bible says the wealth of the wicked is laid up for the just, God doesn't steal passwords to transfer funds that way. Certainly it's true that the wealth of the wicked is laid up for the just, but that's not how it will happen. God is not a thief; the devil is the thief who "comes to steal, kill, and destroy" (John 10:10).

But if you trust Him, God will teach you how to prosper and how to deal wisely in all the affairs of this life. God will help you pay off things early. God will bless you with jobs, raises, bonuses, investments, settlements and inheritances. God will bless you financially by giving you ideas and wisdom. There's no end to the number of ways God can and will prosper you. If He has to, God will send you a fish with a coin in its mouth (Matthew 17:27).

Philippians 4:19 says, "...My God shall supply *all your need* according to his riches in glory by Christ Jesus." The New Living Translation says of verse 19, "This same God who takes care of me...." That's exactly what our God does—He takes care of us.

Yet when you think about it, salvation and divine healing come from heaven straight to you; they are received spiritually and then manifest or show up on the outside of you. But when you look to God to meet your financial needs or pay your bills, those needs must be met materially down here on earth.

The good news is that angels are ready to work supernaturally right here on earth to help us and bring money to us. We ought to expect angels to work together with us whether we see them or not. We'll talk more in Chapter 10 about how to activate angels and put them to work in our lives, but meanwhile, it's important to realize that every time we step out and speak God's Word for finances, angels go to work bringing money to us.

Shot into the Air Like a Rocket

A friend of mine shared this testimony with me about how an angel helped bring in the money he needed. Some time ago, my friend was encountering very difficult financial problems, and he was in a hotel room praying about the amount of money he needed. All of the sudden, he sensed a presence walk in the room. He looked up, and there was a huge angel standing right in front of him. My friend said the angel didn't say a word, just stood there staring at him.

"I didn't know what to do," my friend said. "I just looked at him." My friend didn't ask, "What are you here for? What do you want? Do you have a message for me from God?" He didn't say a word at first.

Then, without thinking, my friend said right out loud, "My God supplies all of my need according to His riches in glory by Christ Jesus."

Instantly, the angel turned and shot into the air like a rocket. Almost immediately, finances started coming in to meet the need. You see, the angel didn't go to work until my friend gave the angel something to do by speaking the Word. When the Word was spoken, that angel got really busy, really fast.

I figure if that angel went to work for my friend—and God is no respecter of persons—then there's an angel ready to bring money in for me when I speak, "My God supplies all my need according to His riches in glory by Christ Jesus." There are angels ready to supply your need, and the angels know where to go find the money.

"Oh, but, you don't know how much money I need," somebody says. Apparently you don't realize how big your angels are.

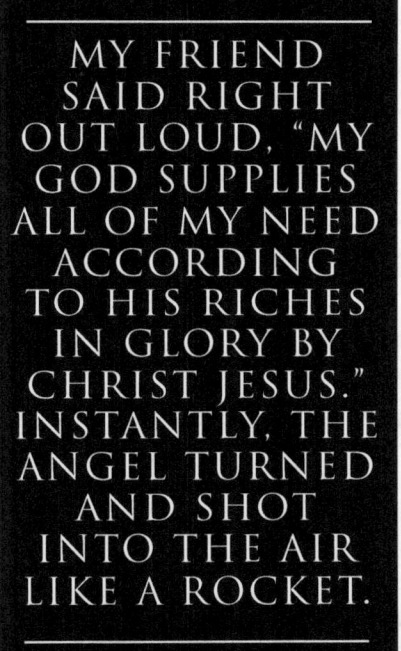

MY FRIEND SAID RIGHT OUT LOUD, "MY GOD SUPPLIES ALL OF MY NEED ACCORDING TO HIS RICHES IN GLORY BY CHRIST JESUS." INSTANTLY, THE ANGEL TURNED AND SHOT INTO THE AIR LIKE A ROCKET.

Finances and Harvest

In these days I believe angels will be increasingly busy bringing money to Christians who tithe and give offerings to spread the gospel. From the beginning God has promised to provide for His children, and from the beginning God has been busy storing up money to finance His latter-day harvest of souls. Let's look at James 5 to understand more about God's harvest account and how angels are involved.

James 5:1-8

1 Go to now, ye rich men, weep and howl for your miseries that shall come upon you.

2 Your riches are corrupted, and your garments are motheaten.

3 Your gold and silver is cankered; and the rust of them shall be a witness against you, and shall eat your flesh as it were fire. Ye have heaped treasure together for the last days.

4 Behold, the hire of the labourers who have reaped down your fields, which is of you kept back by fraud, crieth: and the cries of them which have reaped are entered into the ears of the Lord of sabaoth.

5 Ye have lived in pleasure on the earth, and been wanton; ye have nourished your hearts, as in a day of slaughter.

6 Ye have condemned and killed the just; and he doth not resist you.

7 Be patient therefore, brethren, unto the coming of the Lord. Behold, the husbandman waiteth for the precious fruit of the earth, and hath long patience for it, until he receive the early and latter rain.

8 Be ye also patient; stablish your hearts: for the coming of the Lord draweth nigh.

Do you realize that angels are actually mentioned in the passage above? Before we look at the phrase in detail, we need to lay some groundwork that will help us understand the context.

First of all, we know James is writing to the Church because he tells the *brethren* to be patient. We also know James is talking to the Church about the Second Coming of Jesus, because obviously Jesus had already come to earth and returned to heaven in order for there to be a Church established. So James is telling believers to be patient for Jesus' return, and he's telling believers how to watch for it.

"But wait," somebody says, "Before Jesus can return, Russia has to come down and attack Israel." Or, "We've got to have World War III before Jesus can return." Most people try to figure out when Jesus will return by Bible prophecy alone. However, James gave us something even more sure to watch.

Don't misunderstand me. There's no question that Bible prophecy provides us with a road map and valuable markers to indicate where we are in time. But writing by the Holy Ghost, James provided us with a really specific end-time sign. Look again at verse 7 to understand what the sign is.

> **James 5:7**
>
> 7 Be patient therefore, brethren, unto the coming of the Lord. Behold, the *husbandman waiteth for the precious fruit of the earth*, and hath long patience for it, until he receive the early and latter rain.

The word *husbandman* is not a common word today, and it isn't really clear to us. Most translations replace *husbandman* with the word *landsman*, or better yet, the word *farmer*. In other words, James is saying that if we want to know more about the return of Jesus, we need to watch the farmer. What is the farmer doing in this verse? Actually, what does any farmer do? He finds the best ground he can and plants the best seed he can find in that ground. Then a good farmer waits for the rain to fall and the seed to sprout so He can reap his harvest.

Likewise verse 7 refers to God as the husbandman or farmer, and God cultivates and reaps the same as any other good farmer. God has always believed in the law of seedtime and harvest. God lost fellowship with humanity in the Garden of Eden when Adam and Eve sinned, but He had a plan to restore fellowship through Jesus Christ. He found the best ground available—the world.

Then God planted the best seed the world had ever seen by planting His only begotten Son Jesus into this earth. Jesus called Himself a seed in John 12, saying, "Except a seed of corn fall to earth and die, it abides alone, but if it dies it'll bring forth much fruit."

Now God is waiting for a big harvest that has taken some 2,000 plus years to grow. God is waiting for the precious fruit of the earth, or as one translation says, He's waiting for His "valuable harvest to ripen" (James 5:7 NLT). Notice that the verse did not say that God is waiting for war here or there or a certain country to attack another. No, God is waiting on a huge, massive, enormous harvest of souls that's bigger and grander than anything we've ever seen.

The harvest God has in mind won't include only a few anointed frontier evangelists reaching into the dark corners of the world. The harvest God has in mind will be the Church rising up to take its place with sons and daughters of God really acting like sons and daughters of God.

So what is the catalyst that brings forth the return of Jesus? Harvest. Jesus' return is brought forth by harvest—not war. And harvest will be brought forth by rain falling, which means an outpouring of the Holy Spirit or the manifest presence and glory of God invading the earth. (More detailed teaching about the glory of God is available in a book by Mark Brazee titled *Invasion of Glory*).

Somebody says, "But I thought God's presence already fell on the Day of Pentecost?" Yes, it did, and that was one facet or one degree of His presence, but heaven always has more to pour out. That was only the beginning—not the end. A strong presence of God manifested or tangibly demonstrated itself again during the well-documented Azusa Street revival in the early 1900s. God's presence fell again during the Healing Revival in the 1940s and 1950s and yet again during the Charismatic Renewal in the 1960s. Nevertheless, heaven has plenty more to offer.

Location, Location, Location

Just as God is preparing an outpouring of His Spirit to reap His harvest of souls, God is preparing His harvest account to pay for it all. God has been saving up money in the world's system to finance His harvest.

God is saying, "There's a harvest of souls coming, and it's going to take money to bring in souls. But it's my harvest, and I can afford it. I can pay for it." In fact, I believe every nation has enough wealth to reach its own people; usually the money is simply in the wrong hands.

Bottom line, there's no money shortage and no money problem down here on earth—*only location issues*. Nevertheless, if we'll trust God, He has ways of transferring money from one location to the other. One of the ways God accomplishes this task is to use angels to bring in money and influence people by the will of God.

Let's look at verses 1-3 again.

James 5:1-3
1 Go to now, ye rich men, weep and howl for your miseries that shall come upon you.
2 Your riches are corrupted, and your garments are motheaten.
3 Your gold and silver is cankered; and the rust of them shall be a witness against you, and shall eat your flesh as it were fire. Ye have heaped treasure together for the last days.

If we look at the face value of these three scriptures without combining them with verses four through eight, we might think that God is aggravated with people for being rich. But that's just not true. Let's look at a few more scriptures to help us rightly divide and understand what God is saying.

Consider 2 Corinthians 8:9, where Paul says, "For ye know the grace of our Lord Jesus Christ, that, though he was rich, yet for your sakes he became poor, that ye through his poverty might be rich." If being rich is wrong, then we're all wrong, and it's God's fault because He made us that way.

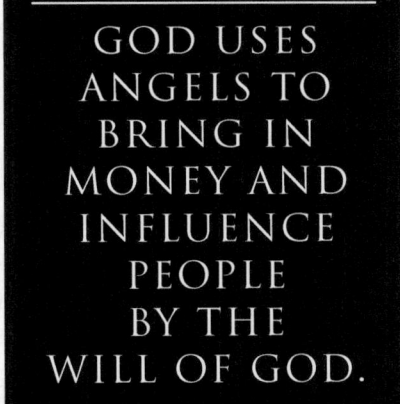

GOD USES ANGELS TO BRING IN MONEY AND INFLUENCE PEOPLE BY THE WILL OF GOD.

Besides, *rich* isn't what we *have*; *rich* is what we *are*. *Rich* isn't what we have in the bank; *rich* is what we became when we were saved. The Bible says that Jesus was made poor for our sakes that we through His poverty might be made rich. *Rich* doesn't mean we've got such-n-such amount in the bank; *rich* means abundant supply. It means that we are connected to a heavenly Father with unlimited supply who will always take good care of us and meet our needs.

God cannot be talking to the rich people in the Church in James 5:2-3 because He made the Church rich. We know God isn't opposed to wealth in the Church because as we study back through scriptures, God instructed the rich to be ready and willing to communicate or to give. He told them not to trust in riches. So if riches were wrong, why would God give rich people instructions on how to live? He would not. Clearly, God is not talking to rich people in the Church.

God *is* talking to the world's rich people. Is He mad at them? No, wealth doesn't bother God. What does matter to Him is what people worship. When you think about it, the gold that an awful lot of people worship here on earth is what God walks on in heaven. What we use for currency, He uses for pavement. God isn't uptight about money like some folks. He doesn't care if the Church is wealthy, and He doesn't care if the world is wealthy. The whole point to God is how money is used.

What did we read in verses 2-3? It said, "Your riches are corrupted, and your garments are motheaten. Your gold and silver is cankered [or rusted through]; and the rust of them shall be a witness against you, and shall eat your flesh as it were fire" (James 5:2-3). *Moth-eaten and rusted through* are signs of what? Inactivity.

God is talking to the rich of the world who've been storing up huge sums of wealth in bank accounts where it does absolutely nothing for anybody. There are folks who have enough money saved up for 20 generations to come. There are people who are so rich they don't even know what to do with themselves or all their money; they have so much money socked away they cannot spend the interest off their money.

In reality, there are some very rich people on this earth, and there are some very poor people on this earth. But there's not a money issue anywhere in the world—it's all a *money location issue*. It doesn't bother God when people have money. But it does bother Him when people have millions and millions stored aside doing absolutely nothing for anybody when He's got a harvest of 7 billion plus souls to reap.

Talking to the wealthy of the world, James 5:3 says, "...Ye have heaped treasure together for the last days." The truth is, the world thinks they've heaped treasure together for *their* last days, but they don't realize what they've done is heap treasure for *the* last days. There's a lot of money in the world's system out there, and God is about ready to call in some of it.

One of the best ways to bring in the wealth of the sinner that's laid up for the just is to bring in the sinner. God doesn't get into people's bank accounts and steal. No, God wants to bring in people who bring their stuff with them and then find out why they're alive on this earth.

One thing for sure, there's plenty of money out there in the world's system and a harvest of the precious fruit of the earth costs lots of money. That's no surprise. The last time I went to an airport to fly overseas, the airline did not invite me to fly free because I was a preacher.

Airlines don't reserve special seats for preachers; we pay as much as everybody else. We also have to pay for hotels, food and vehicles. The gospel is free, but it costs a lot of money to spread the gospel so people can hear it. And it's every Christian's commission to do whatever it takes to spread the gospel because the Farmer is waiting for His harvest.

Store Up Money

Let's look at James 5:4 from another angle to see what it says about the world's system saving up money for the last days.

James 5:4

Behold, *the hire of the labourers who have reaped down your fields*, which is of you kept back by fraud, *crieth:* and the cries of them which have reaped are entered into the ears of *the Lord of sabaoth*.

Notice the phrase *the hire of the labourers*. Actually, instead of the phrase *the hire of the labourers*, we would say the wages or paychecks. So to understand the verse better, it helps to read it this way: "Behold the wages or the paychecks of the laborers, have reaped down your fields."

In verse 4 James is talking about laborers or people working in the harvest—soul winners evangelizing on the streets or missionaries preaching to other nations. He's saying laborers or harvesters have paychecks because there are finances in the world's system that will come over into the church world. He's saying the wealth of the sinner is laid up for the just.

God is preparing to pick up the tab for the harvest, so He can reach the uttermost parts of the earth with the good news of Jesus Christ. God has been storing money since He created this place, and He's going to bring it into the Church to finance His harvest.

Now notice the word *crieth* in verse 4. What or who is crying? The wages or the paychecks are crying. Imagine that. The world has been saying for years that money talks. And now God is up in heaven saying, "The money is talking to me. Your paychecks and your wages are talking to me. The wages are crying out, and I've heard the cry."

God is saying there are plenty of finances in the world's system—more than enough to pick up the tab for the end-time harvest—but the money needs to change hands. The money needs to be transferred from one place to another. The wicked or unsaved have been saving it up, but now it's time that money comes into the hands of the just. How will God do it? I don't know exactly, but I do know that He'll come by it honestly.

Angels Transfer Money

Look now at an important reference to angels in verse 4. Notice the phrase *the lord of the sabaoth*. For years I read that as *the lord of the Sabbath*, but that's not what it says at all. The word *sabaoth* actually means *the lord of the hosts or heavenly host*.

Think about it. James is really telling us that God is the *Lord of the angels*. Isn't it interesting when God instructs us about money coming into the Church to finance the harvest, He refers to Himself as the Lord of the heavenly hosts or angels.

Apparently angels have a lot to do with bringing in harvest finances—bringing finances out of the world's system over into the church system. How would that be? Well, the money won't be coming out of heaven. God won't be raining dollar bills on us. He doesn't have a money tree or a printing press in heaven, and He's not a counterfeiter. No, the money is already down here on earth, and God will use angels to transfer it out of one place into another.

Just watch! We'll see some mighty things take place in the days ahead. We'll see witty inventions, great ideas and creative new businesses and plans. We'll see folks go from having nothing to having huge sums of money coming through their hands. Amazing things will take place. Why? Because God must get money into the hands of those who will fund the harvest in order to reach souls around the world.

> ANGELS HAVE A LOT TO DO WITH BRINGING IN HARVEST FINANCES—BRINGING FINANCES OUT OF THE WORLD'S SYSTEM OVER INTO THE CHURCH SYSTEM.

I'm not talking about angels dropping a bag full of money on your front porch, but angels are assigned by God to help you prosper. In fact, you ought to expect angels to work everywhere in every area of life that pertains to you. If you have a business, you ought to expect angels to bring in clients, bring in customers, bring in patients, bring in whomever and whatever pertains to your business that will bring increase and bless you. Christian business people ought to have folks supernaturally coming in all the time.

I'm not talking about somebody walking up to your front porch with a one-time cashier's check for a million dollars like on the television show "The Millionaire." That was an old show where a rich guy would send his employee to find someone in financial trouble, and then show up at the guy's front door with a million dollar check. That's a nice idea in theory, and don't turn down the check if it happens, but that's not necessarily how it's going to work.

Angels Influence for Good

God has His own unique way of getting it done. God has ways of bringing you business contacts, clients, patients and customer traffic. God has ways of bringing you raises, bonuses, benefits, promotions, inheritances, gifts and increases. How will God bring these things about? He has angels assigned to these tasks and involved in every aspect of prospering you.

What will the angels do? How will they get the money? you wonder. *Will I wake up one day with 10 million dollars sitting in my account? Will I wake up one day with my mortgage paid off?* No, God isn't going to steal and neither are His angelic representatives. God isn't going to cancel out your mortgage or foul up the numbers on your account to pay it off because that would be stealing from the mortgage company. But He will help you pay it off. God is an honest God, and you can trust Him. It's only the devil who cheats and steals to get his way.

"Yeah, but I'm believing God to do some supernatural debt cancellation for me, and I believe He's going to cancel out my car payment, or my boat payment or my credit card payments." You might as well give up. If it steals from someone or harms someone, it isn't going to happen.

How will God bring in money then? If you stop and think about it, angels are already down here, and one thing they will do is influence those who will listen to them. After all, evil spirits influence people to do bad things and make bad choices.

People say all the time, "The devil made me do it." While they're joking to some extent, there's also some truth there because people who sin are influenced by evil spirits. There's also a significant element of cooperation and a good dose of desire behind it on the part of the individual who sins. Evil spirits influence people who listen to them. In fact, the truth usually goes something like this for most people: "The devil made me do it, and I helped him along the way."

Yet clearly, spirit beings have a way of influencing people. Sometimes you'll hear on the news where people who committed terrible crimes or mass murders will say, "I heard voices telling me to do it." Obviously the individuals yielded to those voices, but still there were spirits influencing them. Evil spirits cannot make people do anything, but they sure can exert influence.

So then if evil spirits can influence people to do wrong, angels are godly spirits who can influence people to do right and to do good. I believe angels are out and about all the time influencing people to connect with Christians. Angels don't push people into situations or force them any more than God or the Holy Spirit would. But they influence people and whisper into their ears to get them in the right place at the right time where divine connections are waiting for them.

I believe angels are out and about all the time setting up divine appointments, connections and setups for the believer who's walking with God. I'm convinced angels are out and about and busy drumming up business for Christian business owners. If the business owners are honest, I believe angels influence clients, patients and shoppers to go that direction.

I'm totally convinced that if Christian business owners are harvest-minded and trusting God to meet their needs, then angels are out and about doing all kinds of things to find folks looking for the service the Christian provides and influencing and bringing people who need that service.

Why would God do that? He does it because He loves His children and wants to provide for them, and He does it because it's one way to bring more finances into the church world and finance harvest. *If God can get money through you, then He will get money to you.*

If evil and familiar spirits know things about people and use that information for the devil's benefit, how much more can angels know things about people to help them and not hurt them?

I believe angels are out and about influencing people sitting home on Sunday mornings to connect with a local church where their lives can be changed. "I thought the Holy Ghost did that," somebody said. He does, but so do angels. Why not team up from both sides with a sort of spiritual stereo?

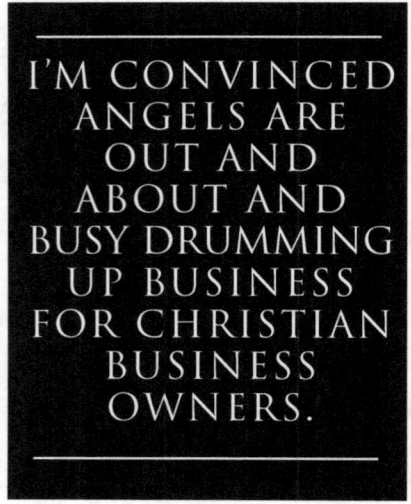

I'M CONVINCED ANGELS ARE OUT AND ABOUT AND BUSY DRUMMING UP BUSINESS FOR CHRISTIAN BUSINESS OWNERS.

We'll talk more in Chapter 10 about how you can activate your angels and get them busy bringing in finances for you. But know this. Every time you speak the Word in faith, angels go to work for you. Every time you say, "My God supplies all my need according to His riches in glory by Christ Jesus," angels go to work bringing in the money.

Chapter Eight

Don't Be Fooled by False Angels

We've focused on several facets of what angels will do, but let's consider what angels won't do. Keep in mind that the world has the topic of angels all goofed up, and since we're about to see a significant increase in angelic activity, it's important that we know the difference between the good, the bad and the ugly on the topic of angels.

We sure can't base our beliefs about angels on movies and television shows because that information is so far off base. There are stories about attractive female angels in long flowing white robes. There are stories about how individuals die, but then hang around as angels until their wings are issued. But these things are not true; they're not in the Bible. The stories may sound innocent, but they're not innocent at all. If you take a good long look into the world's system, you'll see that there are a lot of theories and opinions circulating about angels not supported by the Bible.

The Bible plainly says that for a Christian to be absent from the body is to be present with the Lord (2 Corinthians 5:8). For the person who is not a Christian, to be absent from the body is to be present with the devil. There's nobody hanging around in the middle except evil spirits or demons.

An awful lot of what the world has described as angels really are not angels at all; they're evil spirits fooling people. Somebody says, "Yeah but, I thought evil spirits only did bad stuff." They're willing to throw in some good stuff, too, if it will fool someone into following the devil.

The sad thing is that too many Christians don't take the time to determine the difference between God and the devil and between what is in the Bible and what isn't. Too many people figure if something is supernatural, it must be God, but that isn't Bible truth either.

The truth of the matter is, not all angels are of God. The Bible said in 2 Corinthians 11:14, "…Satan himself masquerades as an angel of light" (AMP). "But besides evil spirits only doing bad stuff, I thought demons were all really ugly," somebody says. They are ugly, but the Bible says they can transform themselves into angels of light or something a little more attractive.

> THE ONLY THING YOU AND I HAVE AS A BOUNDARY IS GOD'S WORD, AND IT NEEDS TO BE THE BOTTOM LINE AND FINAL AUTHORITY ON THE TOPIC OF ANGELS AND EVERYTHING ELSE IN THIS WORLD AND THE SPIRIT WORLD BEYOND.

The only thing you and I have as a boundary is God's Word, and it needs to be the bottom line and final authority on the topic of angels and everything else in this world and the spirit world beyond. We better be Word people and to be Word people means we check everything we hear and read to see if it's in line with the Bible. We need to be as smart as the Bereans in the book of Acts who searched the scriptures to determine if things they heard were so. The closer and closer we get to Jesus' return, the more vital this will be.

Name, Rank and Serial Number

It's so important that we keep the whole topic of angels in perspective. Angels are assigned by God to help the children of God, but as we discussed earlier, we should not worship angels or focus on them; our focus belongs on Jesus.

Some folks have gotten so carried away with angels they begin asking for their names. Should we ask for name, rank and serial number altogether? No, the last I checked, there were no scriptures listing angel names beyond Lucifer who fell and archangels Michael and Gabriel. We don't need to know the names of angels because they're not here to be a major focus of our walk with God. I don't see any Bible precedent where we are to ask angels for their names.

There's also no Bible precedent whatsoever for any other angel to show up and offer its name. All through the New Testament, angels appear to people, but you don't read about them giving their names. Again, the only angels who gave their names in the Bible were Gabriel and Michael, and the Bible has already told us who they are. An angel stood before Cornelius. An angel stood before Philip. An angel stood before Peter and others, but you never read where the angel said, "My name is this or that." The point is, angels that appeared throughout the Bible never focused on themselves in any way.

Angels sent from God will never go outside the boundaries of God's Word because God is His Word, and His Word is the final authority. God won't send angels telling you, "It's good that we have the Bible, but here's more good stuff we can add to it." I'm telling you what, anytime an angel shows up and tells you something that cannot be proven and supported by scriptures, tell the angel to get lost in Jesus' name.

Again, that's why it's so important for the Church—for every Christian—to stay within the boundaries of the Bible. As we approach Jesus' return, I believe we'll see more and more of the supernatural which is all the more reason to be scriptural.

In fact, the Bible makes a real point of warning us about false angels. Notice what Paul said in Galatians 1:6, "I marvel that you are turning away so soon from Him who called you in the grace of Christ, to a different gospel" (NKJV). Then notice what Paul said two verses later.

> **Galatians 1:8-9 (NKJV)**
> 8 But even if we, or an angel from heaven, preach any other gospel to you than what we have preached to you, let him be accursed.
> 9 As we have said before, so now I say again, if anyone preaches any other gospel to you than what you have received, let him be accursed.

Paul knew by the Holy Ghost that there would come a day when false angels would show up and cause problems for believers. As we've already said, it's not as simple as good angels are pretty and do good things while bad angels are demons and do bad things. We cannot necessarily judge by what angels do, we've got to judge by the Bible. God's Word is the bottom line.

False Angels and False Religions

If more folks would go to the Bible to answer their questions about angels, there are major world religions that would not exist today. Other religions pop up because the devil inspires people to look for a way to heaven other than through the blood of Jesus—other than through the death, burial and resurrection of our Savior. Isn't it interesting that there are other religions that do not believe in Jesus, yet they were brought forth by "angels"? Let that soak in for a minute.

One religion is based on a young man who decided to spend time in a cave seeking God, when an angel introducing himself as Gabriel showed up and gave the young man an entirely new gospel. History says that the young man was so upset that he would experience seizures when he would see the angel. That ought to tell us something.

It could not have been an angel of God or an angel of light bringing that message because it brought forth something other than a gospel preaching Jesus Christ as the one and only way to heaven. It preaches something other than the death, burial and resurrection of Jesus Christ. Jesus said, "...I am the way, the truth, and the life: no man cometh unto the Father, but by me" (John 14:6).

I can think of yet another major religion where it's said that an "angel" brought another man a revelation. In this case also, the so-called "angel" mentioned Jesus Christ, but its message did not center on the death, burial and resurrection of Jesus Christ as the only way to the Father.

"But Jesus *is* mentioned," someone points out. Yes, but did you realize that the best and smartest way to kill rats is to mix a little good food with a whole lot of poison? The trick is to use just enough good to disguise the bad. Often times the same principle applies with false religions.

"Isn't any religion that recognizes Jesus still Christian?" someone asks. Does the religion proclaim that Jesus is the way, the truth and the life and that no man goes to the Father but by Jesus? If not, then no. Question answered. We've got to be suspicious of any angelic revelation that offers something new instead of simply expounding on scriptures that already cover everything that needs to be covered. The Bible says there's nothing new under the sun (Ecclesiastes 1:9).

> WE'VE GOT TO BE SUSPICIOUS OF ANY ANGELIC REVELATION THAT OFFERS SOMETHING NEW INSTEAD OF SIMPLY EXPOUNDING ON SCRIPTURES THAT ALREADY COVER EVERYTHING THAT NEEDS TO BE COVERED.

The point is, when it comes to angels, we must be absolutely positive that we remain within the confines and boundaries of God's Word. There's a lot going on in the world right now, and there will be a lot more going on in the future. We will see more and more angel activity.

So remember, angels may be nice and they may seem to do good things, but the Bible must be the final word on the topic. Without the Bible, we won't have the tools to separate the good from the bad and the light from the dark.

Beware!

Awhile back a woman shared a testimony with me about how an evil spirit fooled her into thinking it was good. The woman told me that before she was saved, she had experienced a horrible lifestyle as a teenager. She said at one point an older woman had suggested that a poltergeist could help her through tough times.

"What's that?" she asked the older woman.

"Just ask for one, and you'll find out!" So as a young girl in high school, she went home and said out loud, "I want one of those!" All she did was say those words out loud, and all of the sudden, a young man sat on her dresser talking to her.

As time went on, she said the poltergeist would wait in her room for her every night and tell her what she was doing wrong in life. She thought the being was from heaven because all his conversations focused on how she shouldn't be living like she was; he would make comments to correct her lifestyle.

A few years later, she found out about Jesus and got born again and was doing very well until she went home one day and the poltergeist showed up again. That's exactly what it was—an evil spirit, a demon. She looked at him and said, "I don't need you anymore; I've got Jesus." Just like that he disappeared and never returned.

Without the Bible as our foundation, it's not always so easy to separate and know the difference between light and dark. But, thank God, we can choose to always walk in line with the Bible and reap the benefits of angels of God helping heaven help us.

Chapter Nine

ANGELIC REAPERS OF HARVEST

The closer we get to the Rapture of the Church, the more angelic activity we will see. In fact, as we read back through the gospels, the Bible talks about how the harvest is the end of the age and the angels of God are the reapers of harvest. So as we approach the end-time harvest foretold in the Bible, it will be necessary to see a step up in angelic activity and a flurry of angelic manifestations.

Let's look at Matthew 13 where Jesus was talking to His disciples about the great harvest to come and the role of angels in reaping the harvest. The disciples asked Jesus many questions about the parable of the wheat and the tares, and Jesus gave answers that were important for them and important for us.

One question the disciples asked was, "What's this parable all about?" Jesus answered in the verses below.

> **Matthew 13:37-39**
>
> 37 ...He that soweth the good seed is the Son of man;
>
> 38 The field is the world; the good seed are the children of the kingdom; but the tares are the children of the wicked one;
>
> 39 The enemy that sowed them is the devil; *the harvest is*

the end of the world; and the reapers are the angels.

Particularly notice a portion of the last phrase that says, "...the harvest is the end of the world." Keep in mind that Bible translators chose from a number of different Greek words as they converted the Bible into English. For instance, the phrase *the end of the world* does not mean the end of everything as we know it. It means the end of the age in which we're living. Therefore, Jesus was explaining to the disciples that when harvest comes, it will be the end of the church age.

That tells us a lot. It means as we approach the end of the age, we should expect to see a great harvest of souls because we're going to wrap up this church age in victory. I believe we've come to the kingdom for such a time as this. As for the world, it's in a mess, and the Bible says it will only grow worse. But Jesus was letting us know that at the same time there's a harvest coming that's so big and so grand it will circle the globe. Souls will be saved in places where people have never before heard the gospel; souls will be saved in the uttermost, the regions beyond.

There will be more people getting born again, more backsliders coming back to the Lord, more healings, and more signs, wonders and miracles than anything we've seen before. This end-of-the-age harvest will be the greatest move of God the earth has seen in its entire 6,000-year plus existence.

Angelic Reapers

The Bible also tells us there's going to be plenty of supernatural help with this harvest. Look again at the last phrase of Matthew 13:39 that says, "...the harvest is the end of the world; and *the reapers are the angels.*" Jesus was telling the disciples that the closer we get to the end of the age, the more angelic activity we will see because angels are the harvest reapers.

There are a number of directions we can go with that statement, but we must rightly divide the Word of Truth. Paul wrote to Timothy and said, "Study to shew thyself approved unto God, a workman that needeth not to be ashamed, rightly dividing the word of truth"

(2 Timothy 2:15). Paul would not have made a point of telling Timothy to rightly divide God's Word if it weren't possible to wrongly divide it. That's why it's so important that we really understand the point Jesus was making.

If we take the phrase *the angels are the reapers* at face value, we might come away thinking that Christians don't need to evangelize at all because angels will evangelize for us. In fact, if we roll that thinking all the way out, we might wonder, *My goodness, why should people go through the discomfort of traveling to preach the gospel or living in another nation as missionaries? Why learn other cultures and languages? Why don't Christians just stay home and let angels do the work since angels are the harvest reapers? They don't need money or passports or airline tickets or anything. Wouldn't that be just wonderful?*

> JESUS WAS TELLING THE DISCIPLES THAT THE CLOSER WE GET TO THE END OF THE AGE, THE MORE ANGELIC ACTIVITY WE WILL SEE BECAUSE ANGELS ARE THE HARVEST REAPERS.

No, it wouldn't be wonderful because we wouldn't get to do our jobs. It's not scriptural for angels to preach God's Word. That's not their job—it's ours. You and I are God's mouthpieces. We're the ones who declare and proclaim the gospel. We're the ones who have a great commission—a wonderful privilege—to preach the gospel. Angels are not assigned to do our jobs and cannot do our jobs, but they are assigned to *help* us do ours.

Remember in Acts 10 where we read about Cornelius, the Gentile in the Italian band? He had a group of people at his house who worshipped God, loved God, served God, gave alms to the poor and prayed much. One day when this godly man was praying, an angel showed up and said, "Send to Joppa and get a man named Peter. He'll tell you how you and your house can be saved."

Did you notice the angel did not take the opportunity to preach the gospel to the people? The angel told Cornelius to go find a human to preach the gospel. Why? Because you and I have the privilege of sharing the gospel; angels do not. It's our job as Christians to go into all the world—to our neighbor next door and to the regions beyond—sharing the good news of Jesus Christ.

So what role do angels play in reaping the harvest? If they don't preach, why are they called *reapers* and how will they reap? If we're going to see angels in greater manifestation as we approach the return of Jesus, then what will they be doing?

Angel Winds and Minister Fires

In Hebrews 1 we see how God planned for believers and angels to work together. There's a lot of angelic help that all of us can expect. After all, Hebrews 1:14 says, "Are they [angels] not all ministering spirits, sent forth to minister for them who shall be heirs of salvation?"

Backing up a few verses in Hebrews 1, it says in verse 7, "And of the angels he saith, Who maketh his angels spirits, and his ministers a flame of fire." Of course, we realize that angels are spirits because we don't see them in this natural physical realm. Yet, where the Bible says "*who maketh his angels spirits*," my Bible lists another word in the margin for *spirits*.

Other Bible translations word that verse differently as well. Where it says *spirits* in the King James translation, other translations often use the word *winds*. In other words, the scripture actually says, "...Who maketh his angels *winds*, and his ministers *a flame of fire*."

That's a powerful thought. After all, what does a wind do to a flame of fire? Wind ignites and increases a fire and causes it to spread farther and faster. That natural fact applies to the spiritual realm as well, which is why I believe as we approach the end of the age, we'll see angels increase the spread of the gospel. Angel winds will spread the fire. These supernatural angel winds will cause revival fires to burn hotter, shine brighter, spread farther and travel a whole lot faster.

I'm sure you've heard news reports about forest fires in California and other dry areas. We frequently have warnings here in Oklahoma when things get very dry. Officials sometimes issue red flag warnings so people won't light fires when the wind is blowing because fires can change so dramatically when winds begin to blow on them.

I remember years ago we lived in Broken Arrow, Oklahoma, and I looked out our back window one day to see a flickering light between our fence panels. I stared out the window just long enough to make sure of what I was seeing, and the light flickered more and more. I got right on the phone to report a fire to the fire department, but sadly, by the time the trucks arrived, the house had burned completely to the ground.

The big two story house became a pile of ashes all because somebody in the house left one small candle burning. The small flame wasn't such a big deal until the wind began to blow. A little breeze from an open window blew in and blew the curtains over to the candle. The curtains caught the walls on fire, and the walls caught the ceiling and the floor on fire. Before long the whole house was up in flames and completely consumed by fire. You see, there's no stopping even one little flame when the wind hits it.

> THESE SUPERNATURAL ANGEL WINDS WILL CAUSE REVIVAL FIRES TO BURN HOTTER, SHINE BRIGHTER, SPREAD FARTHER AND TRAVEL A WHOLE LOT FASTER.

Fires are containable until the wind blows and spreads them. When the wind hits a fire, it spreads uncontrollably. You cannot contain it or hold it in, and glory to God, it's the same with the gospel. Men and women are called to preach the gospel, but when supernatural angelic winds begin to blow on the gospel message, it cannot be contained.

You should begin praying right now that a great supernatural wind will begin to blow on your pastor and anyone who steps in the pulpit of your church. Ministers are flames of fire, and angels are the winds that fan the flames. God wants to hook up hand in hand with those who stand to minister and supernaturally equip them to do what they're called to do. God never intended for any of us to do supernatural things naturally.

Notice what the great commission in Mark 16 says about God working with believers:

Mark 16:15-20

15 ...Go ye into all the world, and preach the gospel to every creature.

16 He that believeth and is baptized shall be saved; but he that believeth not shall be damned.

17 And these signs shall follow them that believe; In my name shall they cast out devils; they shall speak with new tongues;

18 They shall take up serpents; and if they drink any deadly thing, it shall not hurt them; they shall lay hands on the sick, and they shall recover.

19 So then after the Lord had spoken unto them, he was received up into heaven, and sat on the right hand of God.

20 And they went forth, and preached every where, the Lord working with them, and confirming the word with signs following. Amen.

When "all ye" go preaching the gospel what will happen? The Bible says the Lord will confirm His Word with signs following. When God tells men and women to preach the gospel, He plans for all of heaven—all the powers of heaven, the winds of heaven and the angels of heaven—to back us up.

Angel Winds Blowing

I'm reminded of a story about the late John Osteen who was the founder of Lakewood Church in Houston, Texas. He could preach more in 20 minutes than most of us could convey in 20 weeks. He preached wonderful messages that would stay with you forever.

Someone sitting in the crowd of one of his services shared this story with me. The person said Brother Osteen was preaching a masterpiece of a message when the presence of God became so thick in the room it seemed as if he could cut it with a knife. The person said the interesting thing was that Brother Osteen would preach a little, then stop. Preach a little, then stop. Preach a little, then stop all through the sermon.

Suddenly, the eyes of this person observing were opened into the spirit realm, and the person saw what was really happening. There was a huge angel standing right behind Brother Osteen on the platform whispering to him as he preached. The person said Brother Osteen would preach, and the angel would lean over and whisper into his ear. Then Brother Osteen would take off preaching again. The person said it was the most amazing thing, and it happened over and over again because the angel was giving him the sermon to speak.

I thought right then, *Those are the kind of sermons I want to give!* Sometimes when I pause during a message, I think I'm trying to find my place again, but I would like to think it's actually an angel giving me more inspired points. Hallelujah! If you're called to stand in a pulpit and preach, thank God for angel winds to help increase the message. I'm convinced that as ministers of the gospel, we ought to be expecting angels to team up with us and help us whether we see them or not, whether we hear them or not, whether we know they are there or not.

God has lots of supernatural help for every one of us no matter what we're called to do. Every one of us ought to be expecting angelic help around the clock because angels ought to be magnifying and increasing what God has us doing for Him in the earth.

Whether we're in a pulpit capacity or a believer capacity, anyone ministering to people is a flame. So we can expect angelic winds to blow on us anytime we're doing something in a ministry capacity, whether it's cleaning the church or directing cars in the church parking lot. Anytime we're doing anything that will help people to receive the Word of God easier and better, we can count on angels to connect with us. If we're doing our jobs right and doing the best we can, angels will hook up with us and enable us to do our jobs better, easier and faster.

Flames of Fire

There's another facet of this topic I want us to consider. Look with me again at Hebrews 1:7, which says, "...Who maketh his angels spirits, and his ministers a flame of fire." There's another way to interpret the phrase *his ministers a flame of fire*. Actually, you can take that phrase a couple of different directions.

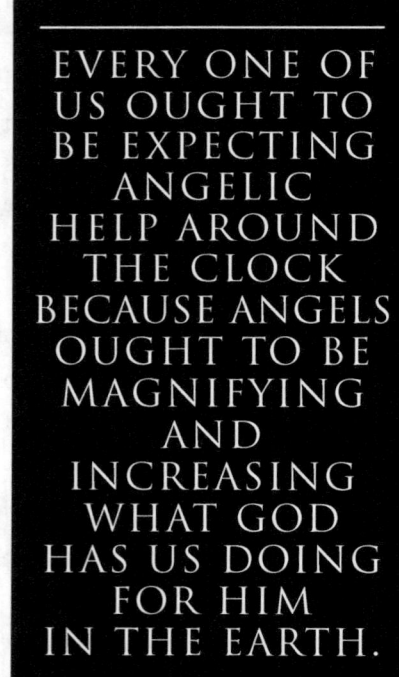

> EVERY ONE OF US OUGHT TO BE EXPECTING ANGELIC HELP AROUND THE CLOCK BECAUSE ANGELS OUGHT TO BE MAGNIFYING AND INCREASING WHAT GOD HAS US DOING FOR HIM IN THE EARTH.

In modern-day English, we usually refer to ministers as one of the five-fold ministry gifts listed in Ephesians 4 such as apostle, prophet, evangelist, pastor or teacher. Those are definitely the ministry gifts as we know them, and yet, the word *minister* in most languages doesn't mean pulpit gift at all. In most languages, the word *minister* means *servant*. That casts a different light on things, doesn't it?

For example, when we started our DOMATA school network worldwide to train ministers, we prayed about a name that would translate well into any language. Initially, we planned to call them Minister's Training School of whatever country where the school was located. Yet almost invariably in every language that name translated as Servant's Training School, which was confusing. A lot of folks thought we were training servants to work in people's homes. Actually, to a degree we were.

So when the Bible tells us that "his ministers are flames of fire," we could focus on what we call pulpit ministers. Or, we could just back off and use the word *servants* for the word *ministers*. That would translate: God makes his servants flames of fire and his angels spirits or winds. In other words, *angels will work for those who work for God.*

Paul gave us a similar example by calling himself a bond servant of the Lord Jesus Christ. In times past, a bond servant was a slave who had been given freedom from his or her master. But then, the bond servant loved his or her master so much he or she would turn around and say, "You gave me my freedom, but I want to give you my life."

To seal the deal, so to speak, the bond servant would poke a hole in his or her ear lobe. Then anytime folks saw a person with a big hole in the ear lobe, they realized the person was a bond servant who had been given freedom but chose to give his or her life back.

Paul was saying, "I'm a bond servant of the Lord Jesus Christ. I was a slave to sin. Jesus gave me my freedom, but I loved Him so much I gave my life back to Him. I was bought with a great price, and now I am not my own any more. I belong to Jesus Christ." Really even though the Bible calls us sons or daughters of God, we should also be servants—bond servants.

Whatever we do as servants, God has equipped us with angelic help to do it better. We may do well on our own as a child of God and a servant of God, but we'll do even better when angels hook up and help us. Remember what happens when the winds hit a flame?

I read awhile back about fires raging so furiously in California that they burned up some 60 million dollars worth of homes in what seemed like no time at all. Officials later explained that they had been containing the fire with some success until the wind hit. Then nothing could stop the fire. No wonder God said He would send His angel winds to ignite His servants.

Angels Unawares

The Bible mentions something else about angels in Hebrews 13 that's not limited to Bible days. Verse 2 says, "Be not forgetful to entertain strangers: for thereby some have entertained angels unawares."

Using more modern language, The New Living Translation says, "Don't forget to show hospitality to strangers, for some who have done this have entertained angels without realizing it."

I had an encounter like this more than 20 years ago that I still remember. Janet and I were on the road traveling from church to church ministering at that time, and one particular night I left our hotel room fairly late to pick up something from a grocery store. I purchased the item and got back in my car to leave the parking lot.

As I started the engine, a man walked up to the car window. When I rolled down the window, he asked if I could spare a couple of dollars. It was one of those situations where I thought to myself, *Get a job!* But I said, "No, not right now." I rolled the window up and drove off.

But I got as far as the edge of the parking lot and thought, *Something isn't right.* So I circled back and drove around looking for the guy. It was one of those experiences where I had chills go up and down my back, and I sensed that I had just missed a really good opportunity. Somehow it seemed to me that he might have been an angel.

"Now do you really think God would have an angel in a parking lot bumming money off people?" somebody asks. I don't know, but I've always had the funny feeling that I missed it. I'll tell you this. From that time on, when somebody comes up to me in a situation like that asking for money, I stop and check on the inside before I say no. I won't miss another good opportunity to be a blessing to an angel down here or anyone else God wants me to help.

That does not mean we should give money to everyone who comes along begging for it, but we do need to be led by the Holy Spirit and not just automatically write everyone off either. It *could be* an angel.

Years before I had a similar incident. Late one night in another city, I was headed home after a meeting in a downtown building. As I walked across the parking lot, there was a guy sitting on the pavement playing the guitar with his case open next to him. To be honest, he wasn't playing very well, and I remember thinking, *That boy will starve if he thinks he's going to make money off his music.* I'm no musician, but let's say he was in need of some serious lessons of some sort; it was that bad.

All the sudden, I got a quickening down on the inside. This incident was 30 years ago and $20 was a little more than $20 is now, and it's still plenty. But I just had an unction to throw a $20 bill in his case while he was strumming his guitar.

"You cannot do that!" he said immediately as he stopped his playing. "That's too much!"

"No, it isn't," I said. "I really believe God wanted me to do that." The door was wide open, and I got a chance to witness to him. In fact, I would say that was $20 well spent.

The book of Hebrews tells us to be hospitable, and I believe we can be led by the Holy Spirit as we're hospitable. That doesn't mean that across the board we should hand out money to everyone and anyone, but it does mean we need to be led by the Holy Spirit. There are times we could be entertaining angels, or as it said in the King James Version, *angels unawares.*

When the Bible says *unawares,* it means we would be unaware. Therefore, that must mean that in these sorts of situations, it would not be obvious to us that a person was actually an angel. These incidents will probably be ones that make us want to ask, "If they are angels, why would they need our money or our help?" The answer is, I don't know. I don't have this all figured out. All I know is that the Bible says we're supposed to be hospitable because there will be times when angels need our assistance.

We need to be led by the Spirit of God in all the affairs of life. But as we approach the last days, I suggest that we especially be aware of angels unawares.

Chapter Ten

ACTIVATING ANGELS IN YOUR LIFE

Most people have barely tapped in to the angelic help available to us. Yet, this is a topic we need to know more about because we sure don't want a company of angels sitting around a camp fire singing "Kumbaya." We've got billions of souls to reach down here on earth, and we need every angel busy. I sure don't want the angel assigned to me sitting on the sidelines when I need help. There's too much work to be done for angels to sit around with no directions.

We need angels helping with harvest and bringing in souls. We need angels protecting Christians. We need angels bringing direction and instruction. We need angels delivering healings and miracles. We need angels bringing in money and divine connections, customers, clients, patients and whatever we need in business. We need angels working with us in whatever we're doing in the will of God. We're the flames, and they're the wind, and we need to count on them.

"If it's God's will, it will happen," somebody says. No. The body of Christ has already been there on a few topics. That's like saying, "If it's the will of God, I'll get saved or healed." No, you and I always have something we must do in order to receive from heaven.

Can you imagine God walking by a couple of million angels sitting on the sidelines in heaven? He would probably walk by a time or two and say, "Hey, why are you guys sitting around doing nothing anyway?" Then can you imagine a couple of million angels answering Him, saying, "We tried to get busy, God, really we did. But the Church won't give us anything to do." Somehow I don't think God would be too happy about that.

THE BIBLE GIVES US EVERY REASON TO EXPECT A GREAT STEP UP OR INCREASE IN ANGELIC ACTIVITY, SO WE NEED TO GET OUR ANGELS BUSY.

We're close to the Second Coming of Jesus, and the Bible gives us every reason to expect a great step up or increase in angelic activity, so we need to get our angels busy. "Well, I can hardly wait for it to happen," somebody says. You don't need to wait for it to happen. You can activate angelic help right now. In fact, God's Word outlines specific ways you can activate and deactivate angels.

A Prime Way to Activate Angels

We need to take these instructions seriously because a lot of times we're not getting the results we're supposed to get or want to get, and we're not getting the manifestations God wants in our lives because we don't give assignments to our angels the way God instructs.

Let me ask you a question. Suppose you hired 10 people to work on your house or on your lawn, but they showed up and sat down with their hands folded in your front yard. Suppose you walked by and only said, "Hi! How ya doin'?" They would probably still be sitting there.

If you don't tell workers what you want done, they have no instructions to act upon. Workers cannot do what you want if they don't know what you want, and it's the same with angelic activity in our lives. Too often we haven't had angels working for us because we have not given them work to do.

Let's take a look at Psalm 103:20 that shows us the primary way to activate angelic help in our lives.

> **Psalm 103:20**
> Bless the LORD, ye his angels, that excel in strength, that do his commandments, hearkening unto the voice of his word.

Pay close attention to that last phrase. Did you notice the scripture does not say that angels hearken to God's voice, though I'm sure they do. No, the scripture specifically says that angels hearken to the voice of God's Word.

What's the difference? Actually, there's a huge difference. This scripture is telling us that angels go to work and get busy when voice is given to God's Word. That means they go into action when somebody—like you and me—speaks the Word.

You cannot just wave your Bible at them. You cannot just hope they know what you need. But every time you make a bold declaration from God's Word in faith, angels take off to hearken to the voice of that Word and bring it to pass in your life.

Let me come at this from another direction. Angels don't fly into action because you own a Bible or even because you faithfully read your Bible. Angels don't go to work for you simply because you have a Bible sitting on your coffee table. Just because you once read a scripture,

> EVERY TIME YOU MAKE A BOLD DECLARATION FROM GOD'S WORD IN FAITH, ANGELS TAKE OFF TO HEARKEN TO THE VOICE OF THAT WORD AND BRING IT TO PASS IN YOUR LIFE.

doesn't mean angels are bringing it to pass. It doesn't happen that way. No, angels get busy when you give voice to God's Word; *they hearken to the voice of it.*

The Bible says when you open your mouth and give voice to God's Word, then—and only then—angels will get busy on your behalf. "What happens if I don't say anything?" Nothing! "What happens if I say something inspirational, but I don't speak the Word?" Nothing at all happens. The Bible says angels hearken to the voice of God's Word—not just *any* word.

Every time you give voice to the Word of God, angels grab those words and run out to get busy. Your words load your angel with ammunition to help you. Every single time you speak God's Word, you can bank on the fact that angels just went to work in your behalf.

Every time you speak out, "I am the head and not the tail. I am above and not beneath. No weapon formed against me can prosper. Since God be for me, who can be against me? God sent His Word and healed me and delivered me from my destructions. The steps of a good man are ordered of the Lord," you are giving directions to a host of angels.

"Yeah, but doesn't God give them directions?" Certainly! God gives angels instructions, but you also gave angels directions when you spoke the Word. Who did? *You did!* You declared the Word of God, and it sent angels hurrying into action. After all, God created angels to minister to you and for you—so they're waiting on your instructions.

Let's say you confess out loud Philippians 4:19, saying, "My God supplies all my need according to His riches in glory by Christ Jesus!" Angels hearken to the voice of the Word, and they take off collecting finances in your behalf. Your angels are probably rubbing their hands together saying, "Ok! Now I've got something to do!"

But what if the next day you say, "Well, I don't see any money yet. I guess this confession business doesn't work. God never works any miracles for me. I've never had an extra dime in my life, and I guess it won't be any different now." What happens? You just took your angels off their assignment. You assigned angels when you spoke the Word, but you unassigned them when you spoke the opposite of the Word. You activated them, and then you deactivated them.

Now don't go praying for some ridiculous figure and say, "Well, I need a trillion dollars." That's fine, but it won't happen unless you've got your own printing press. The truth is, it's not a matter of what God can do anyway; it's a matter of what you can believe.

Have you got trillion-dollar faith? I didn't think so. Then pick out something you know your faith can handle. Then when that amount comes in, move on to bigger and better things. I've watched these instructions for finances work in my life for more than three decades now. It still works all the time, and it always will.

But now remember in Chapter 7 where we talked about my friend who was praying about financial difficulties in his hotel room and an angel showed up staring at him? As soon as my friend spoke out, "My God supplies all of my need according to His riches in glory by Christ Jesus," immediately the angel took off like a rocket. Finances almost immediately started coming in to meet the need.

That angel was obviously assigned by God to help my friend, and yet, the angel wasn't in action, wasn't activated, wasn't working until my friend gave the angel something to do by *speaking the Word*. The angel showed up in my friend's hotel room, but just stood blinking at him. The angel wasn't out working to get finances in my friend's behalf; the angel was waiting. What was the angel waiting on? He was waiting *for my friend to speak God's Word—waiting until voice was given to God's Word.* Why? Because angels *hearken to the voice of God's Word.*

God's Word spoken in faith activated angelic help. That means there are angels ready to supply your need as well because God is no respecter of persons. There are angels on standby ready to bring in the money you need. Psalm 103:20 says they are mighty. They excel in strength. And they know where to go find the money.

Prayer Activates Angels

Another important avenue to activate angels and get them working in your life is prayer. Your prayers open the door for angels to get busy helping you. Being a person of prayer and walking in the supernatural always go hand in hand.

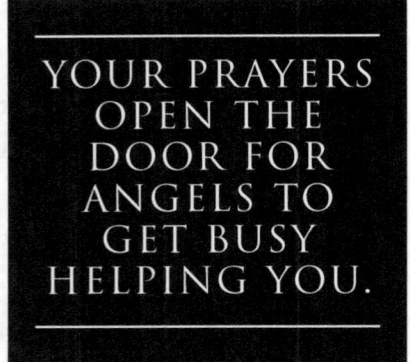
YOUR PRAYERS OPEN THE DOOR FOR ANGELS TO GET BUSY HELPING YOU.

Remember in Acts 12 when Peter was thrown into prison? Herod had already killed James with the sword, and next he wanted to take off Peter's head. But the Bible said the church went to instant and earnest prayer, and it paid off.

The early church didn't just pray a quick little prayer like, "Lord, bless Peter. Take care of him in Jesus' name. Amen." No. They *prayed* and *stayed* with it. There are some kinds of prayers we can pray one time, believing we receive the answer when we pray. But there are other kinds of prayer where we must stay with it, which is something we've lost in the Charismatic world. We've lost the art of praying down heaven. We've lost the art of what old time Pentecostals called "praying through."

"Are you supposed to 'pray through' to God?" somebody asks. No, you're already "through" to God. You have to pray through what hell has tried to array against you, but that's another subject in itself.

It's obvious in the case of Peter that the early church prayed and stayed with their prayers. How do we know? We know because an angel broke Peter out of jail, and Peter walked right up to the prayer room and knocked on the door. The church members were so busy praying for Peter they didn't even answer the door, which is what I call fervent prayer. That's not praying for 10 minutes with one eye open. Man, they stayed with their praying until they had victory—until they had Peter.

What we need to see here is that being a person of prayer activates angelic activity. It's amazing what God can accomplish in your life and mine if we'll maintain a strong prayer life. Listen to me, though. The goal isn't to pray for angels or to pray for God to send angels—the goal is to pray that the job gets done. How it gets done is up to God.

I don't see where the early church prayed for an angel to help Peter. I don't see where they prayed earnestly for God to break Peter out of jail. What I see is that the Church prayed for God's help, and God decided *how* to help. If the Church will pray, God will figure out what kind of heavenly back up is needed.

Daniel's Prayers

Daniel is another example of a man who was greatly helped by prayer. In Daniel 10 it says that he had some serious situations going on in his life and needed information about the future, so he began praying, praying, praying. All of a sudden, he looked up and an angel was looking right straight at him.

But did you notice that Daniel was not praying for an angel? He was praying for results, but one of the ways God brought results was through an angelic visitation. I'm telling you what, there's something important about our prayer lives. If we'll maintain a strong prayer life and be faithful to give voice to God's Word, there's no limit to what God can do to help us in times of need.

Hezekiah Prays Down Victory

In 2 Chronicles 32, there was an Assyrian king named Sennacherib who led a vicious army to attack Jerusalem. He was a fierce enemy and a mouthy one, too. Let's read more about him here below.

> **2 Chronicles 32:1-5 (NKJV)**
>
> 1...Sennacherib king of Assyria came and entered Judah; he encamped against the fortified cities, thinking to win them over to himself.
>
> 2 And when Hezekiah saw that Sennacherib had come, and that his purpose was to make war against Jerusalem,
>
> 3 he consulted with his leaders and commanders to stop

the water from the springs which *were* outside the city; and they helped him.

4 Thus many people gathered together who stopped all the springs and the brook that ran through the land, saying, "Why should the kings of Assyria come and find much water?"

5 And he strengthened himself, built up all the wall that was broken, raised *it up* to the towers, and *built* another wall outside; also he repaired the Millo *in* the City of David, and made weapons and shields in abundance.

Sennacherib, a conquering king who came from a long line of conquering kings, was marching through the countryside taking cities and villages. This time Sennacherib was on his way with his armies to romp and stomp all over Jerusalem. King Hezekiah had trouble breathing down his neck.

Sennacherib bragged that no enemy had ever been able to withstand his armies. He taunted the people in Jerusalem, yelling, "Don't listen to your King Hezekiah. He'll just tell you about a God who cannot do anything. We've been attacking city after city, and their gods didn't help them. Yours won't be able to help you either. What makes you think your God can help you anyway?"

> IF WE TAKE CARE OF THE NATURAL, GOD WILL TAKE CARE OF THE SUPERNATURAL. WHERE WE LEAVE OFF, GOD PICKS UP.

The Assyrian King was pushing on some bad territory by hollering at the city of Jerusalem like that. But he just kept shooting off his mouth saying, "You're God can't help you stand against me. I'm bigger than He is for sure."

King Hezekiah took this enemy seriously. First he started out doing everything he knew to do in the natural, and there's nothing wrong with that. He repaired the city, built up the wall and strengthened defenses. He also made a good strategic move and cut off the water supply so the enemy outside the city wouldn't be able to get water.

King Hezekiah did every smart thing possible in the natural realm. That's what we also should do, confident that God will do the rest. If we take care of the natural, God will take care of the supernatural. Where we leave off, God picks up. We do an easy thing; God does the hard thing. We do a possible thing; God does an impossible thing. What we cannot afford to do is sit around and do nothing.

We read earlier about how the angel in Acts 12 who had to kick Peter and tell him to wake him up and put his shoes on in order to break him out of jail. There's a real point there. You see, the angel didn't suspend Peter in mid air, put his shoes on, wrap him up in his coat and then carry him out. No, the angel said, "Hey, Peter, wake up! Get up! Get your shoes on! I'll open the door!"

I think a lot of times we're expecting God to do everything, when really God expects us to do everything we know to do. Faith is the primary thing we know to do. God didn't say He would do everything for us. God said, "With God all things are possible." He steps into the impossibilities after we do the possibilities.

In Hezekiah's situation, he had done everything he knew to do, and He made every natural provision. We can learn a lot from him about what to do in a tough situation. Have you been in one of those?

Notice the next few verses.

> **2 Chronicles 32:6-7 (NKJV)**
> 6 Then he [King Hezekiah] set military captains over the people, gathered them together to him in the open square of the city gate, and gave them encouragement, saying,
>
> 7 "Be strong and courageous; do not be afraid nor dismayed before the king of Assyria, nor before all the multitude that *is* with him; for *there are* more with us than with him.

Hezekiah had tended to everything in the natural, and then he set about tending to the spiritual. He had something to say. Verse six said he gathered the people in the open square and encouraged them. He extended his faith to the citizens of Jerusalem and told them,

"OK, now, we've done our part. We've got the walls fixed. We got everything ready to go. We're in the midst of a battle here, but we've done everything we know to do."

Then he says, "Let me tell you ahead of time. Don't be bugged by this mouthy guy. Don't let the number of them bother you either because those with us are more than those against us." What was he doing? Hezekiah was making a public declaration of his faith and confidence in God.

Then the next verse says:

> **2 Chronicles 32:8 (NKJV)**
> With him [Sennacherib] is an arm of flesh; but with us is the LORD our God, to help us and to fight our battles." And the people were strengthened by the words of Hezekiah king of Judah.

In other words, Hezekiah told his people, "Don't be afraid! All this guy has is an arm of the flesh. We have Almighty God, El Shaddai, the All Sufficient One. God is with us, guys! This is not a problem!"

The truth is, if God will deliver His children in the Old Testament, God will do it again in the New Testament. He'll do it again today for you and me. Sometimes we look at a battle and think, *This is a tough one*. It would be if we had to fight it, but the battle is not ours—it's the Lord's. All we need to do is get that message through our heads because Jesus has already conquered the enemy, and He's already won the victory. All we have to do is collect the spoils.

Notice what happened next.

> **2 Chronicles 32:9-10 (NKJV)**
> 9 After this Sennacherib king of Assyria sent his servants to Jerusalem (but he and all the forces with him *laid siege* against Lachish), to Hezekiah king of Judah, and to all Judah who *were* in Jerusalem, saying,
> 10 "Thus says Sennacherib king of Assyria: 'In what do you trust, that you remain under siege in Jerusalem?

Let's read these scriptures beginning with verse 9 out of The Message, which makes them even clearer.

> **2 Chronicles 32:9-10 (The Message)**
> Later on, Sennacherib, who had set up camp a few miles away at Lachish, sent messengers to Jerusalem, addressing Judah through Hezekiah: "A proclamation of Sennacherib king of Assyria: You poor people—do you think you're safe in that so-called fortress of Jerusalem? You're sitting ducks.

Have you felt like this before? Have you ever gotten to the place where you've done everything you know to do? You're standing on the Word of God, declaring the Word of God and believing the Word of God. But the devil comes playing with your mind like you're a sitting duck, saying, "You're crazy. You really think this stuff will work? Do you really think God will bail you out of this one? You're in deeper than you've ever been before. Man, you're a fool."

Have you ever had the devil talk to your mind like that? Sure you have. We all have, and here in these verses Sennacherib, a devil in the flesh, was talking the same way:

> **2 Chronicles 32:11 (The Message)**
> Do you think Hezekiah will save you? Don't be stupid—Hezekiah has fed you a pack of lies.

The devil is such a liar. He's probably told you, "That preacher you listen to is just giving you a lot of hot air. You know you've had this genetic ailment come on you, and it's been in your family for generations. You're ready for bankruptcy this time. You got yourself into this mess, and there's no way out. Even God cannot get you out of this one. Nobody can help you this time." The devil likes to taunt you just like Sennacherib taunted Hezekiah in this next verse.

> **2 Chronicles 32:12 (The Message)**
> When he says, 'God will save us from the power of the king of Assyria,' he's lying—you're all going to end up dead. Wasn't it Hezekiah who cleared out all the neighborhood

worship shrines and told you, 'There is only one legitimate place to worship'?

In other words, Sennacherib is telling the people of Jerusalem that Hezekiah took away all their idols and all their gods and left them with nothing but the one true God. Sennecherib thought that was bad; Hezekiah knew it was good. Do you get the opinion that Sennacherib didn't know who he was dealing with, and he's in for a big surprise?

> **2 Chronicles 32:13 (The Message)**
>
> Do you have any idea what I and my ancestors have done to all the countries around here? Has there been a single god anywhere strong enough to stand up against me?

This guy really dug himself a deep hole. "Do you know not one single god has been able to stop me?" he says. The guy just keeps going on and on, digging deeper and deeper.

> **2 Chronicles 32:14-15 (The Message)**
>
> Can you name one god among all the nations that either I or my ancestors have ravaged that so much as lifted a finger against me? So what makes you think you'll make out any better with your god?
>
> Don't let Hezekiah fool you; don't let him get by with his barefaced lies; don't trust him. No god of any country or kingdom ever has been one bit of help against me or my ancestors—what kind of odds does that give your god?"

Sennacherib really had a mouth on him. But there's a showdown coming, because I'm telling you, the more the devil pushes, the more God says, "Back up. I'm going to show off."

> **2 Chronicles 32:16 (The Message)**
>
> The messengers felt free to throw in their personal comments, putting down both God and God's servant Hezekiah.

Can't you just imagine all the Assyrian King's servants echoing him like little imps, saying, "Right on, king!" "You tell 'em, king!" "Go for it, king!" "Yes, king!" "You're always right, king!"

> **2 Chronicles 32:17-18 (The Message)**
> Sennacherib continued to send letters insulting the GOD of Israel: "The gods of the nations were powerless to help their people; the god of Hezekiah is no better, probably worse." The messengers would come up to the wall of Jerusalem and shout up to the people standing on the wall, shouting their propaganda in Hebrew, trying to scare them into demoralized submission.

Have you ever had the devil taunt you and scare you into demoralized submission? Have you had the devil try to just plain wear you out, beat you down and tell you that you're crazy? Has he told you that you won't get out of a problem or you cannot be healed? Has he told you that you'll never make it out of a financial mess? Well, keep reading!

> **2 Chronicles 32:19 (The Message)**
> They [the enemy] contemptuously lumped the God of Jerusalem in with the handmade gods of other peoples.

That wasn't a smart move. Now, notice. The Assyrian King was harassing and intimidating the people of Jerusalem. He was bragging that his army had whipped everybody else, and he was reminding them, "Nobody's ever been able to lift a finger against me. They couldn't, their gods couldn't, and your God probably can't either."

Then what happened? King Hezekiah had made his declaration of faith, and he did not back off of what he believed. He did everything he could do in the natural to prepare. And Hezekiah also reached a point where he had heard just about all he wanted to hear from the mouthy Assyrian king. Sometimes we've had all we can stand, and we can't stand any more.

So what did King Hezekiah do? Look at verse 20.

> **2 Chronicles 32:20 (The Message)**
> King Hezekiah, joined by the prophet Isaiah son of Amoz, responded *by praying, calling up to heaven.*

When everything looked its worst and the devil was screaming, "I'm going to take you down, and there's nothing you can do about it," Hezekiah decided it was time to make a call. Hezekiah had done what he could in the natural realm he had declared what he believed for all to hear. Then he prayed—***calling up to heaven.***

What happened?

God answered the call! And God sent an angel to take care of things. Notice the next verse.

> **2 Chronicles 32:21 (The Message)**
> *GOD answered by sending an angel* who wiped out everyone in the Assyrian camp, both warriors and officers.

God didn't just shut up the enemy; He wiped them out. God's children didn't even fight. They didn't have to go to battle. They didn't have to pick up a sword, a spear, a shield or anything else. They just began to pray. They called heaven, and God answered.

How did God whip the enemy?

God sent an angel.

I'm telling you, if only one angel could wipe out an entire army, both warriors and officers, imagine what a host of angels could do. Is anything too hard for our God?

Hezekiah declared and prayed, and heaven responded with angelic help. Notice what the next verse says.

> **2 Chronicles 32:21 (Message)**
> Sennacherib was forced to return home in disgrace, tail between his legs. When he went into the temple of his god, his own sons killed him.

I guess we could say that Sennacherib had a bad day. Then again, he never should have talked about our God the way he did. He never should have made the mistake of lumping our mighty God in with all the other false gods and the little handmade gods.

With natural ability and strength, it wasn't possible to defeat Sennacherib's army—no army had done it for generations and no other god was able to do it either. But all of sudden there was Hezekiah saying in essence, "This one thing I do know. I do know whom I have believed and am persuaded that He's able to keep that which I have committed unto Him against that day."

> HEZEKIAH CALLED HEAVEN FOR HELP. GOD ANSWERED THE CALL! AND HE SENT AN ANGEL TO TAKE CARE OF THINGS.

Hezekiah made a declaration and told his people, "Don't worry. Everything will be all right. We serve a big, great, Almighty God. Just chill. Relax. It's not your problem." Then when Hezekiah and the prophet began to pray, God sent an angel to wipe out the entire army. God sent the Assyrian king home with his tail between his legs, and the king's own sons finished him off.

Hezekiah prepared. Hezekiah declared. Hezekiah prayed. And God answered. These are the same important things we can do to effectively loose angels to work in our behalf.

I believe the body of Christ is right on the edge of a move of God that's been a long time coming, and I'm convinced we're about to see a flurry of angelic activity on the earth like never before. But here's the truth of the matter. It won't happen just because we're nice people. It won't happen just because we obey God's Word. It won't happen just because we declare the Word of God in the midst of impossible-looking situations. But it will happen when we believe God's Word, declare God's Word and pray.

"But you don't understand," somebody says. "It just doesn't look like there's any way out of the mess I'm in." It doesn't matter what your situation looks like because the real truth is *Jesus' middle name is way.* He's Jesus—*the way,* the truth and the life. "I *am* the way!" He said. It's not a street. It's not an avenue. The way is a person, and His name is Jesus. So when there seems to be no way, just remember there *is* a way, and He lives in you and me. And He promises to deliver us out of *all* our destructions.

> WHAT BROUGHT HELP ON THE SCENE FOR HEZEKIAH WILL BRING HELP ON THE SCENE FOR YOU, NO MATTER WHAT SITUATION YOU FACE.

What worked for King Hezekiah will work for you. What brought help on the scene for him will bring help on the scene for you, no matter what situation you face. Hezekiah declared the Word and prayed, and what happened? God answered and sent an angel. That's how Hezekiah activated angelic help, and that's how *you* can activate angelic help.

I don't see from God's Word where it's our job to speak directly to angels and assign them tasks. But what do I see from the Word is that God expects us to speak the Word and pray, and God will disburse the assignments. What I see is that God has more than enough angels to help you however you need help.

Angels on Go

Recently, I heard about some folks who had a ministry project rolling in their hearts that they wanted to accomplish for God. They sensed God was dealing with them, but they were looking for how to step out and obey.

Before long the couple had a vision, and in the vision they saw themselves exploring how to launch out and serve God in this certain area of ministry. They saw themselves walking around and around in the vision absolutely surrounded by angels.

Then, still in the vision, they saw themselves take steps and move forward with this ministry assignment. When they did, the many, many angels all stood up with great energy. There was great expectation and intensity on the faces of the angels, and it was obvious they were alert, determined and ready to go into action.

Yet, still in the vision, this couple would think, *Oh, man, this project would be good, but it would require a lot of work and a lot of resources. Should we really do this after all?* As the couple thought this way, they would find themselves turned around walking in the other direction. When they did, all the angels would sit back down.

This went on a few times back and forth and back and forth. When the couple thought of launching out, the angels all stood up with great determination and intensity ready to get busy, but every time the couple turned around all the angels would sit down again.

This vision makes an interesting point to us all. As long as we're going forward with the plan of God for our lives—whatever God tells us to do—then we're surrounded with help from heaven. As long as we're declaring God's Word and praying, we're surrounded with angels ready to help us, ready to minister to us and for us. They're ready to make things happen. They're ready to bring guidance. They're ready to protect us. They're ready to arrange divine appointments and connections. They're ready to bring in provision and money, and they're ready to deliver us however we need delivering.

Our angels don't plan to sit around in heaven and cheer from the balcony. They don't plan to sit in the grandstands eating popcorn and hollering down, "Go saints! GO!"

What do our angels plan to do?

They hearken to the voice of God's Word and the voice of prayer.

So let's speak God's Word!

Let's pray!

Let's get our angels busy bringing help from heaven.

Putting Angels to Work in Your Life

The first step toward putting angels to work in your life is receiving Jesus Christ as your Lord and Savior. We read in Hebrews 1:14 that God has assigned angels to minister to and for the heirs of salvation, and you can become a joint-heir of Jesus by praying this simple prayer aloud. It will be the most important decision you've ever made.

> Dear heavenly Father: Your Word says, "Whosoever shall call on the name of the Lord shall be saved" (Acts 2:21). I call on You right now.
>
> The Bible also says if I confess with my mouth that Jesus is Lord and believe in my heart that You have raised Him from the dead, I shall be saved (Romans 10:9-10). I make that choice now.
>
> Jesus, I believe in You. I believe in my heart and confess with my mouth that You were raised from the dead, and I ask You to be my Lord and Savior. Thank You for forgiving me of all my sins. I believe I'm now a new creation in You. Old things have passed away; all things have become new in Jesus' name (2 Corinthians 5:17). Amen.

If you prayed this prayer today, please share the good news with us!
Mark Brazee Ministries
P.O. Box 470308
Tulsa, OK 74147-0308
918-461-9628 // prayer@woctulsa.org

Mark Brazee Ministries
REACHING THE WORLD
The Word • The Spirit • The World

Find the multi-media format convenient for you!

BOOKS – Teaching materials by Mark Brazee available at www.brazee.org.

TELEVISION – "Experience God with Mark Brazee"
National and International broadcast listings at www.brazee.org

RADIO – "The Spirit-Led Life with Mark Brazee"
Broadcast via the Internet, Tulsa and northeastern Oklahoma with listings available at www.brazee.org.

WORLD OUTREACH CHURCH

Senior Pastor Mark Brazee
For more information, location and service times, visit www.woctulsa.org or call 918.461.9628.

Live streaming and archived services of Pastor Mark Brazee are available at www.woctulsa.org.

www.ingramcontent.com/pod-product-compliance
Lightning Source LLC
LaVergne TN
LVHW051604070426
835507LV00021B/2759